"Sinclair Ferguson knows how to write deep theology that helps simple people like me. And there is no deeper topic than the Advent of our glorious Lord in this broken world. *The Dawn of Redeeming Grace* is written by a wise author offering us rich insights, so that we journey more confidently from this world to that which is to come."

RAY ORTLUND, Renewal Ministries, Nashville

"It is hard not to be a little envious of Sinclair's uncanny knack of unpacking familiar material in a manner that causes one to say, 'Why didn't I see that?' These short readings have helped me read my Bible with fresh insight, and in the process my heart has been strangely warmed."

ALISTAIR BEGG, Senior Pastor, Parkside Church, Cleveland;
Bible Teacher, Truth for Life

"For many of us, the road through the Christmas story is very familiar territory: so familiar that we have a hard time seeing it through fresh eyes. In *The Dawn of Redeeming Grace*, Sinclair Ferguson is a worthy and helpful guide, pointing out insights we may have missed and guiding us toward wonder and worship."

NANCY GUTHRIE, Author and Bible Teacher

"Walking Matthew's narrative path with magnifying glass in hand, Sinclair Ferguson points out easily missed details and overlooked shifts in the plot. *The Dawn of Redeeming Grace* shows us what happens when God keeps his word to rescue lost humanity. Let's follow the path to our own Advent discoveries."

SHERIDAN VOYSEY, Author, *The Making of Us*;
Presenter, Pause for Thought on BBC Radio 2

"As Christmas gets more and more secularized, trivialized and sentimentalized (even in the evangelical church), we need a heavy dose of thinking deeply about the arrival of the Son of God. Sinclair Ferguson provides the spiritual riches that your heart longs for as you contemplate the birth of our Savior."

JOHN MACARTHUR, Pastor and Teacher, Grace to You

"With fresh insight, Sinclair Ferguson unpacks the doctrine of the incarnation. A highly recommended read in the weeks leading up to Christmas. It will do your heart good!"

GAIL CURRY, Baptist Women's Director, Association of Baptist
Churches in Ireland

Silent night, holy night!
All is calm, all is bright
Round yon virgin mother and child!
Holy infant, so tender and mild,
Sleep in heavenly peace,
Sleep in heavenly peace.

Silent night, holy night!
Shepherds quake at the sight:
Glories stream from heaven afar,
Heav'nly hosts sing, "Alleluia!
Christ the Saviour is born,
Christ the Saviour is born!"

Silent night, holy night!
Son of God, love's pure light,
Radiant beams from thy holy face
With the dawn of redeeming grace,
Jesus, Lord, at thy birth,
Jesus, Lord, at thy birth!

Joseph Mohr (1792-1848)

THE DAWN OF
REDEEMING
GRACE

SINCLAIR B.
FERGUSON

The Dawn of Redeeming Grace
© Sinclair B. Ferguson 2021

Published by:
The Good Book Company

thegoodbook.com | thegoodbook.co.uk
thegoodbook.com.au | thegoodbook.co.nz | thegoodbook.co.in

ISBN: 9781784986384 | Printed in the UK

Cover Design by Faceout Studio, Molly von Borstel.
Design and art direction by André Parker

CONTENTS

Part Three: The Visitors

Part Four: The Journeys

INTRODUCTION

They say time is relative, and it can certainly seem that way as Christmas approaches. To a busy parent—with presents to wrap, cards to send, meals to prepare, and spare batteries to remember to buy—time seems to fly. There is not enough of it—and there is simply too much to do. But to a child, the days of December seem the longest in the whole year; they pass more slowly than the last few miles of a tedious journey. No wonder C. S. Lewis's description of Narnia as a land where it was "always winter but never Christmas" resonates with children. They do not need to go through the back of a wardrobe to feel that—all you do is turn the calendar to the month of December!

Today's children are not the first to think that Christmas can't come soon enough. Indeed, that was the feeling of generations of Old Testament believers: a feeling picked up in the words of Charles Wesley's hymn "Hark! The Herald Angels Sing":

Late in time behold him come,
Offspring of the Virgin's womb.

"Late in time"? Jesus came late?

Our own experience sometimes gives certain words an atmosphere unique to ourselves. Perfectly innocent words can have a chilling effect on our emotions! For me, "late" is one of them. I cannot hear it without feeling that I am being accused! Perhaps it is because I can still hear in my mind the shrill voice of one of my teachers shouting at me, "Ferguson, you're late" (when I wasn't!). With that kind of memory, it is hardly surprising that to me the phrase "late in time" has a somewhat negative ring about it.

Was Jesus also "late"? No, Wesley did not mean Jesus came at the wrong time. But since God's people had been hoping for his coming ever since the divine proclamation of Genesis 3:15 had promised the arrival of one who would bruise the serpent's head, it must have seemed a very long time. The believers of the Old Testament were often heard crying out, "How long, Lord?" Would it always be winter but never the long-promised Christmas?

When it has been my responsibility to arrange the items of praise for the first Sunday in Advent, I have always chosen to begin with a 12th-century hymn that captures this sense of waiting and longing:

O come, O come, Immanuel
And ransom captive Israel,

That mourns in lonely exile here
Until the Son of God appear.

O come, Thou Rod of Jesse, free
Thine own from Satan's tyranny;
From depths of hell thy people save,
And give them victory o'er the grave.

Rejoice! Rejoice! Immanuel
Shall come to thee, O Israel.

God may seem slow, but he is always on time. He has never been late. But if you read through the Bible from the beginning, there is something thrilling about turning over the blank page between the Old Testament and the New Testament. The first thing you encounter is Matthew's summary of the long years of waiting (1:1-17). But now the snow is melting, and winter is giving way to Christmas (1:18 – 2:23). The arrival of the Lord Jesus is the dawn of a glorious new era.

Matthew's Gospel begins with two chapters on the nativity. It may seem strange that he does little more than mention the actual event of that first Christmas Day. ("She had given birth to a son," 1:25, and "After Jesus was born…", 2:1; that is all he says.) But he has his reasons. Births take place every day of the year, ever hour of the day. But this birth was different, and Matthew wants to spend most of his time helping us to understand why it was.

As this Christmas approaches, I invite you to join me in exploring what Matthew says about those days that marked the dawn of redeeming grace and about how Christ's light breaks into our lives today.

I am grateful to The Good Book Company for allowing me the rare privilege of writing a book that perhaps many thousands of people in different parts of the world will read simultaneously, even reading the same pages on the same days. By doing so, we become a great company of individuals united by the shared experience of reflecting on Matthew's account of the birth of Jesus. It is the prologue to the greatest story of all—the story of Jesus. And it is one that will make many millions sing Joseph Mohr's famous lines again this Christmas:

> *Silent night, holy night!*
> *Son of God, love's pure light,*
> *Radiant beams from thy holy face*
> *With the dawn of redeeming grace,*
> *Jesus, Lord, at thy birth!*

My prayer is that as you read, you will experience "the dawn of redeeming grace" because "Christ the Saviour is born."

Sinclair B. Ferguson

PART 1

THE FAMILY
HISTORY

Matthew 1:1-17

¹The book of the genealogy of Jesus Christ, the son of David, the son of Abraham.

²Abraham was the father of Isaac, and Isaac the father of Jacob, and Jacob the father of Judah and his brothers, ³and Judah the father of Perez and Zerah by Tamar, and Perez the father of Hezron, and Hezron the father of Ram, ⁴and Ram the father of Amminadab, and Amminadab the father of Nahshon, and Nahshon the father of Salmon, ⁵and Salmon the father of Boaz by Rahab, and Boaz the father of Obed by Ruth, and Obed the father of Jesse, ⁶and Jesse the father of David the king.

And David was the father of Solomon by the wife of Uriah, ⁷and Solomon the father of Rehoboam, and Rehoboam the father of Abijah, and Abijah the father of Asaph, ⁸and Asaph the father of Jehoshaphat, and Jehoshaphat the father of Joram, and Joram the father of Uzziah, ⁹and Uzziah the father of Jotham, and Jotham the father of Ahaz, and Ahaz the father of Hezekiah, ¹⁰and Hezekiah the father of Manasseh, and Manasseh the father of

Amos, and Amos the father of Josiah, [11] and Josiah the father of Jechoniah and his brothers, at the time of the deportation to Babylon.

[12] And after the deportation to Babylon: Jechoniah was the father of Shealtiel, and Shealtiel the father of Zerubbabel, [13] and Zerubbabel the father of Abiud, and Abiud the father of Eliakim, and Eliakim the father of Azor, [14] and Azor the father of Zadok, and Zadok the father of Achim, and Achim the father of Eliud, [15] and Eliud the father of Eleazar, and Eleazar the father of Matthan, and Matthan the father of Jacob, [16] and Jacob the father of Joseph the husband of Mary, of whom Jesus was born, who is called Christ.

[17] So all the generations from Abraham to David were fourteen generations, and from David to the deportation to Babylon fourteen generations, and from the deportation to Babylon to the Christ fourteen generations.

1. IN THE BEGINNING

The first words of a book are important. They can make you read it or make you close it!

Some time ago I began to read the biographies of two contemporaries who were on opposite sides of the American Revolution. One biography began with an explanation of the subject's complex family tree and varied royal connections; the other with these words:

> *In the cold, nearly colorless light of a New England winter, two men on horseback travelled the coast road below Boston, heading north.*[1]

You can guess which book I kept reading. The first quickly lost my interest. Family connections can be very confusing and—at least outside the family—are interesting to only a few. But I wanted to know more about the two men on the Boston coast road; who were

---

1 David McCullough, *John Adams* (Simon & Schuster, 2001), p 17. In the interests of full disclosure, the book is prefaced by a double spread of the Adams family tree!

they and why were they there in the first place? My attention was captured immediately (and sustained to the last page).

The opening section in Matthew's Gospel isn't exactly an attention-grabber for most of us. It is a long list of largely unfamiliar names. Some of them we may not even be sure how to pronounce. We don't usually read this part of Matthew in Christmas services!

But these opening words would have grabbed the attention of Matthew's first Jewish readers and hearers (and most of them were hearers). Literally they read, "Book of [the] genesis of Jesus Christ, son of David, Son of God." To a certain generation, "Genesis" is a famous band from the 1980s and 90s; but for Matthew's audience "genesis" meant "beginning." It is the name of the first book of the Bible, the story of the original beginning.

This word choice was not accidental. Matthew's book is the story of a new genesis—of a new beginning. His Gospel, and indeed the Christian gospel message as a whole, is about God establishing his kingdom and beginning what Paul called a "new creation" (2 Corinthians 5:17).

Matthew's Gospel has sometimes been described as "The Gospel of the kingdom." He tells us how Jesus taught about "the kingdom," how his miracles were signs of its presence, and how he explained the new and different lifestyle of its members (Matthew 4:23 – 7:29). Matthew also ends his Gospel with an indication of Jesus' kingship. Jesus' last words to the apostles are these: "All

authority in heaven and on earth has been given to me…"
(28:18). Now his rule will be extended to the ends of the
earth and to the close of history.

The gospel story is all about how Jesus Christ, the son
of David, in God's kingdom restores life to what it was
meant to be. In other words, it is about a new genesis.

Think back to the original creation. In that first beginning, God created mankind, male and female, as
his image and likeness. He said, "Let them have dominion…" (Genesis 1:26). They were royal children
appointed to reign over the kingdom of creation. But
Genesis tells the story of their tragic fall from that privi-
leged role. Their calling was to turn the dust of the earth
into a garden (1:26 – 2:25). Instead, they sinned and
became part of that dust themselves (3:17-19).

But now, as we stand in the opening pages of Matthew's Gospel, God is bringing about a grand rever-
sal. The whole story of the Old Testament has been a
preparation for it. Now the new beginning has begun.
What follows will tell the story of how Jesus undid the
effects of Adam's fall, and accomplished what Adam
and we have failed to do. The result will be a "new creation": what Matthew calls "the new world" (Matthew
19:28)—literally the *palingenesia*—the beginning again!

So, Matthew's opening words are good news for
anyone who needs a new beginning. That's why his
Gospel ends with Jesus telling his apostles (who were
all Jews) that they were to go to the ends of the earth
with the message that the dominion, and authority,
and the kingdom of God, have all been restored. Christ

has inaugurated a new genesis in which all who come to faith in him will share.

But still, we're left with the question: why then this seemingly endless list of names?

The answer lies in the three ways in which Matthew describes Jesus.

First, Jesus is the Christ. Matthew mentions this fact four times here (1:1, 16, 17, 18). "Christ" is the Greek equivalent of the Hebrew word "Messiah," meaning the anointed King whom God had promised to send to deliver his people from bondage. That's who Jesus is.

But Jesus is also the son of David (1:1). Why is that important? Because God had promised that a descendant of David would reign over a kingdom that would stretch from one end of the earth to the other. That king would restore the world Adam marred.

And Jesus is also a son of Abraham (1:1). For even earlier God had promised that this same person would be descended from Abraham, and in him all the nations of the earth would be blessed—they would experience the blessing that Adam had forfeited through his sin (Genesis 12:1-3).

There is more to come in Jesus' genealogy. It isn't at all what you might expect. But that will need to wait. For today let us ponder the fact that Advent is all about the new beginning God has made possible by sending his Son for us.

Perhaps a new beginning is what you need most. As you reach the end of another year, is there some aspect of the previous twelve months in which you wish you could start over? If so, Matthew wants you to know that you can find that new beginning in Jesus Christ.

Earth was waiting, spent and restless,
With a mingled hope and fear;
And the faithful few were sighing,
"Surely, Lord, the day is near;
The desire of all the nations,
It is time he should appear."

Earth for him had groaned and travailed
Since the ages first began,
For in him was hid the secret
That through all the ages ran—
Son of Mary, Son of David,
Son of God, and Son of Man.

"Earth was Waiting, Spent and Restless"
Walter Chalmers Smith (1824-1908)

Lord Jesus, you came into the world so that we might have a new beginning. Thank you that your word assures us that everyone who belongs to you becomes part of a new creation. Work in us your new creation so that your kingdom may come in our lives. Amen.

2. "THE HOPES AND FEARS OF ALL THE YEARS"

Looking at the list of names in Matthew 1:1-17, you could be forgiven for wishing Matthew had simply said, *Jesus was descended from David and Abraham!* You can barely take it all in. Matthew is cramming almost 2,000 years of Bible history into 16 verses—over 100 years per verse! 42 generations are listed. Most of us don't even stop to check his arithmetic. It is hard to concentrate on so many names that mean almost nothing to you.

But pause for a moment and you will realise Matthew is telling us something. He has sorted the names into three groups of 14 generations each: from Abraham to David; from David to the Babylonian exile; and from the exile to Christ. Why?

And—since we know from elsewhere in the Bible that there were more than 42 generations between Abraham and Jesus—why does Matthew abbreviate them? And why three groups of 14? It looks like a deliberate pattern. But what does it mean?

One attractive explanation is that to Matthew's Jewish readers, the number 14 had special significance.

Numbers often have significance for us too. The jerseys of famous sportsmen used to have only their team number, not their name, on the back. Simply to say the number was virtually to say the player's name. To most moviegoers today, "007" means only one thing: James Bond.

To a Hebrew who loved numbers, 14 might well seem significant: it was King David's number! In Hebrew his name was written D-V-D, using the consonants *dalet* (D), *vav* (V), *dalet* (D). In antiquity letters also denoted numbers (even today we might write the year 2021 using "Roman numerals" or letters: MMXXI). In the Hebrew alphabet *dalet* is the fourth letter; *vav* is the sixth letter. D-V-D therefore is 4 + 6 + 4 = 14.

Matthew goes out of his way to make the point that the number of generations is significant. In case we miss it, in verse 17 he tells us three times, *Notice the 14 generations.* So did his first readers hear "David, David, David" playing in the background to these verses?

Whether or not this link with David is the right way to understand Matthew's threefold division of Jesus' genealogy, it is undoubtedly part of his message. It is the first thing he says about Jesus. He is "the son of David." The angel who appears later in Joseph's dream seems to underline it. He reminds Jesus' adoptive father that he is "Joseph, son of David."

So, Matthew identifies the central figure in his book in several ways. Four times he tells us that his name is

Jesus (1:1, 18, 21, 25). Four times we are told he is the Messiah (1:1, 16, 17, 18). And the genealogy as a whole focuses on his *royal identity as son of David.*

The message? Jesus is the legal heir to the throne of David. This is the family tree of Israel's greatest king. God had made a covenant with him promising that from his line the Messiah would come. On his deathbed David confessed his faith in God keeping that covenant: "He has made with me an everlasting covenant, ordered in all things and secure" (2 Samuel 23:5).

At times (as the genealogy indicates), that covenant promise seemed doomed. But now Matthew has traced it to an artisan's home and to Jesus. He is the promised king. News of his reign will spread to the ends of the earth and to the end of time (Matthew 28:18-20). God's long-awaited King has come; his kingdom is about to be established as that of David's legal heir.

There were times during Israel's history when God seemed to have forgotten his promise or even appeared to have been destroying it himself (as numerous psalms eloquently lament). God's people felt that he had shunted them into a cul-de-sac and left them there. Yet this genealogy shows us that God was keeping his promise all the time, from beginning to end.

Perhaps this explains why, in Matthew's Gospel, Jesus' genealogy moves *forwards* from Abraham to Jesus rather than *backwards* from Jesus (as in Luke 3:23-38). Matthew's message is this: from the very beginning God knew exactly where he was going. Throughout the centuries he was directing history towards this moment.

Despite his people's failures and trials, despite various cataclysmic events (like the exile in Babylon), the longest-standing and most difficult-to-keep promise of God has come to fulfilment in Jesus.

What a lesson for us! Matthew is painting on the large canvas of history a picture of God's sovereignty and faithfulness. But God is no less trustworthy when he paints his purposes on the smaller canvas of our own lives.

We sometimes get lost; but God is never lost. We are often confused by our circumstances; God never is. We have doubts about his purposes; God knows what he is doing. His promises never fail. God may seem slow to us, but he is always moving his purposes on at exactly the right speed. God is never late. He is always on time. And his timing is perfect.

In the coming of the Lord Jesus, God has kept his promise to bless the nations through Abraham's seed (Genesis 12:1-3). Therefore, we can trust him to keep his promises to us too—promises to work for our good, to be with us by his Spirit, and to bring us home to be with him in glory for ever. For "all the promises of God find their Yes in him. That is why it is through him that we utter our Amen to God for his glory" (2 Corinthians 1:20).

Amen?

O little town of Bethlehem,
How still we see thee lie!
Above thy deep and dreamless sleep
The silent stars go by;
Yet in thy dark streets shineth
The everlasting Light;
The hopes and fears of all the years
Are met in thee tonight.

"O Little Town of Bethlehem"
Phillips Brooks (1835-1893)

Lord God, every time we say "amen" help us to remember that you have kept the longest-standing and hardest-to-keep promise of all by sending the Lord Jesus to die for our sins and to rise in triumph to be our Lord. Help us to have confidence that you will keep all your promises to us. Amen.

3. CHERCHEZ
LA FEMME?

"**C**herchez la femme." Literally, this French phrase means "Look for the woman." But as an idiom it means, "If there's a problem, then a woman will always be at the root of it." That, of course, is more than a little unfair. No one ever said "Cherchez l'homme," even although men constitute approximately half of the human race!

But when it comes to the genealogy of Jesus, "Cherchez la femme" is good advice. Women are mentioned only occasionally in biblical genealogies (as in 1 Chronicles 1:32, 50). Usually these family trees take the form "X [the father] begat Y [the son]" and make no mention of the mother. What sticks out in Matthew's account of Jesus' genealogy is that it mentions *five* women altogether. There must be a reason for this. And why only *these* women? After all, *every man* listed had a mother.

The question to ask is this: what do the following women have in common? Tamar (Matthew 1:3); Rahab (1:5); Ruth (1:5); and the wife of Uriah the Hittite (1:6).

For one thing, they were probably all non-Israelites. They didn't naturally belong. For another, there were question marks over their lives: Tamar gave birth to the twin sons of her father-in-law, Judah (the sad story is told in Genesis 38:1-30); Rahab was a Jericho prostitute (Joshua 2:1); Ruth was a Moabitess (Moabites and their descendants were permanently barred from the congregation of Israel, Deuteronomy 23:3); Bathsheba, the wife of Uriah the Hittite, was the object of King David's adultery (2 Samuel 11).

Luke doesn't mention these women in his genealogy of Jesus. So why did Matthew draw attention to these skeletons in the cupboard? I suspect he is giving us hints of three important biblical principles:

1. God extends his grace beyond the chosen people and brings Gentiles into his covenant;

2. God overcomes the effects of sin and shame as he works out his purposes; and…

3. God keeps his promises in ways we could never have anticipated.

The first principle is present in Matthew's Gospel like a pair of bookends. He begins by mentioning these Old Testament "outsiders" who were brought into Jesus' family history and goes on to tells us about more outsiders—wise men from the east—who visited him after he was born. Matthew concludes with Jesus commanding the apostles to go to outsiders—indeed to "all nations" (Matthew 28:18-20).

The second principle reminds us that Christ understands what it means to have sin and shame in our family story.

Jesus did not come into a squeaky clean world any more than we do. He came into a fallen world, and into a family that had blots in its history. He did so out of love for us, and everything we learn about him proves that he is able to sympathise with us.

Whatever it is that causes us shame—from sin or abuse in our past to painful memories that continue to linger—the Lord Jesus understands. He does more than merely see the burdens we privately carry; he has experienced them himself. He was "made like his brothers in every respect, so that he might become a faithful and merciful high priest ... we do not have a high priest who is unable to sympathize with us in our weakness ... Let us then with confidence draw near ... that we may receive mercy and find grace to help in our time of need" (Hebrews 2:17; 4:15-16).

It was to save the kind of people who appear in his family tree that Jesus came. The apostle Paul learned that: "The saying is trustworthy and deserving of full assurance, that Christ Jesus came into the world to save sinners, of whom I am the foremost" (1 Timothy 1:15).

The third principle reminds us that God never loses control of his purposes. True, like the psalmists, we sometimes feel that he has. But when we do, we need to say to ourselves, "Remember Jesus' genealogy!"

God's ways may seem hidden from us, and we may feel we are in the darkness. But "if I say, 'Surely the darkness shall cover me, and the light about me be night,' even the darkness is not dark to you; the night is bright as the day, for darkness is as light with you" (Psalm 139:11-12). God sees as clearly in the dark as in the day; he knows what he is doing and where he is going. He can even weave the dark threads of man's evil deeds, tragedies, and disasters into his purposes and use them for his glory.

Tamar, Rahab, Ruth, Bathsheba—and yes, eventually the young virgin Mary too—would not have been able to see what God would ultimately do through their lives. So it is in every age and for every believer. But God sees the end from the beginning.

If I had been with Matthew when he was writing his Gospel, I would have been tempted to say, "Matthew, please don't begin with a long family tree. It will put most people off reading the rest of the story!" But I am glad that he did because written into his genealogy is this message: God keeps his promises; he knows what he is doing; he knows exactly where he is going; and he is able to rescue us even from past sin and shame.

In what corners of your heart and mind do you need to remember that today?

Child in the manger, Infant of Mary,
Outcast and Stranger, Lord of all,
Child who inherits all our transgressions,
All our demerits on him fall.

Once the most holy Child of salvation
Gently and lowly lived below;
Now as our glorious mighty Redeemer,
See him victorious o'er each foe.

Prophets foretold him, Infant of wonder;
Angels behold him on his throne.
Worthy our Saviour of all our praises;
Happy for ever are his own.

"Child in the Manger"
Mary Macdonald (1789-1872)
Translated by Lachlan MacBean (1853-1931)

Lord Jesus Christ, you were yourself an outsider when there was no room for you in the inn. You had nowhere to lay your head and even in death were laid in a borrowed grave. Thank you that although you were rich, you became poor for our sake so that through you we might become rich. Amen.

PART 2

THE PARENTS

Matthew 1:18-25

[18]Now the birth of Jesus Christ took place in this way. When his mother Mary had been betrothed to Joseph, before they came together she was found to be with child from the Holy Spirit. [19]And her husband Joseph, being a just man and unwilling to put her to shame, resolved to divorce her quietly. [20]But as he considered these things, behold, an angel of the Lord appeared to him in a dream, saying, "Joseph, son of David, do not fear to take Mary as your wife, for that which is conceived in her is from the Holy Spirit. [21]She will bear a son, and you shall call his name Jesus, for he will save his people from their sins." [22]All this took place to fulfil what the Lord had spoken by the prophet:

[23]"Behold, the virgin shall conceive
    and bear a son,
        and they shall call his name Immanuel"

(which means, God with us). [24]When Joseph woke from sleep, he did as the angel of the Lord commanded him: he took his wife, [25]but knew her not until she had given birth to a son. And he called his name Jesus.

4. A VIRGIN CONCEPTION

Traditional Christmas Eve services often begin with the words spoken by the shepherds after they were told that Christ had been born: "Let us now go even unto Bethlehem, and see this thing which is come to pass, which the Lord hath made known unto us" (Luke 2:15; the Authorised/King James Version has a special ring about it, doesn't it?) The service leader often follows the quotation with an invitation to the congregation to join the shepherds and "go to Bethlehem".

Try as I might, I have never managed to arrive—you cannot get to the manger from Scotland!

I don't mean to spoil Christmas Eve services! The invitation sounds spiritual enough and is certainly well-intentioned. But we don't discover the meaning of Christmas by imagining ourselves "there and then." We need to understand it, and see its significance for us, in the here and now. Many people were "there and then" during our Lord's life and it made no difference to them.

But when we begin to understand the significance of that first Christmas, it can have a disturbing effect on us. In fact, it did on everyone in Matthew's story.

It all begins in a matter of fact way: "Now the birth of Jesus Christ took place in this way. When his mother Mary had been betrothed to Joseph..." So far, so good. But then comes the bombshell: "*Before they came together* she was found to be with child" (Matthew 1:18).

Joseph was "betrothed" to Mary. Getting engaged in Western culture isn't the equivalent. Betrothal was more the equivalent of taking your marriage vows. It was a legal covenant that could only be broken by divorce—not simply by handing back the ring. In Joseph's world it had personal, familial, social, and even financial repercussions.

The betrothal period usually lasted about a year. But unlike in an engagement today, a betrothed couple would not spend any time together on their own. So, when Joseph discovered that Mary was expecting a baby, it must have shaken him to the core of his being.

How exactly was Mary "found to be with child"? We can only imagine Joseph's moment of awful realisation. Did he *see* the bump? Did he *work it out* because he heard that Mary was feeling sick in the mornings? Did *her parents tell him* and explain she had gone to stay with her cousin Elizabeth? Or did *Mary* manage to send him a message?

Matthew probably tells us more than Joseph knew at this stage by saying Mary was "with child *from the Holy Spirit*". All Joseph knew was that there was a baby on the way. He was left to his sense of shock, disappointment, and horror because he knew he was not the father. Everything he had believed about Mary was turned upside down. He had believed that she was a deeply spiritual young woman. (Luke makes that abundantly clear in his Gospel.) But this? Pregnant?

We know that everything was going to be ok. But Matthew's point is that it wasn't ok for Joseph. His thoughts about Mary, his plans and hopes for their future, and—no matter what he did now—his own reputation and his family's social standing—lay in tatters around him. He could no longer trust Mary. And if his assessment of her had been so badly mistaken, how could he ever trust himself and his decisions again? Whatever the story of his past (was he, as some have believed, a young widower with children, now with sorrow added to sorrow?), the future must have seemed lonely and bleak.

But view this scene from another angle. For this is the story of how Joseph came to receive Jesus Christ into his home, into his life, and into his heart. It is a glimpse into the way the heavenly Father was preparing him to nurture his incarnate Son. And, as is often true in both Scripture and the history of the church, the man God uses he first bruises. Joseph was being cast completely on the Lord.

Once again, God was writing in capital letters the same story that he writes in smaller letters in many of our lives. When Christ comes, he turns lives upside down and inside out. He changes everything. And these chapters tell us that this was true not only for Joseph and Mary but for wise men, for a king and his court, and indeed for an entire city.

The same may well have been true for you when you first encountered the living Christ. You discovered things about yourself that you didn't want to know: that you were a sinner; that the person you had ignored or despised or opposed was the Saviour you needed. Your view of yourself, your life, your future, the things that mattered most to you—all came under threat. You had this in common with Joseph: you did not understand at the time that God was at work to prepare you to receive Christ.

This pattern is repeated in Scripture. Jacob needed to be wounded by the angel of the Lord if he was to walk into the sunrise (Genesis 32:22-32). Joseph had to be brought low in Egypt before he could be God's instrument of both provision in the famine and reconciliation in his family (Genesis 37 – 50). Isaiah discovered that he, Jerusalem's most eloquent prophet, was a man of unclean lips before he could speak with power of the Holy One of Israel (Isaiah 6). Simon Peter had to sink to his knees in order to be able to lift Jesus high (Luke 5:8).

What about you? In what ways has the Lord graciously brought you low—in the past or in some way right now—in order to use you for his purposes? Yes, God may weave this pattern into your life in a quieter way, in more subtle colours. But if we are ever going to receive Christ as our Saviour, we need to discover that we are sinners. And if we are to yield to him as Lord in every part of our lives, we must first discover our inability to rule them ourselves. What was true for Joseph son of David remains true for us.

⸻

One day when heaven was filled with his praises,
One day when earth was as dark as could be,
Jesus came forth to be born of a virgin—
Dwelt among men, my Redeemer is he.

Living he loved me, dying he saved me,
Buried he carried my sins far away,
Rising he justified, freely for ever;
One day he's coming, O glorious day!

"One Day When Heaven Was Filled with His Praises"
John Wilbur Chapman (1859-1918)
Altered

⸻

Lord, you have promised that you do not afflict us willingly but only to draw us closer to yourself. We pray that, being brought to an end of our own resources, we may gladly welcome Jesus as our Saviour and Lord and find all we need in him. Amen.

5. A WAKING NIGHTMARE

We left Joseph plunged into an emotional night-mare. Matthew adds a further twist: "Joseph, being a just man and unwilling to put [Mary] to shame, resolved to divorce her quietly" (Matthew 1:19).

Joseph was a just man. He was *dikaios*, the same Greek word used of Elizabeth and Zechariah in Luke 1:6, where it is translated "righteous." In the Bible a righteous person is someone who belongs to God's covenant family, receives his blessings, and lovingly seeks to obey his laws and statutes.

Much of whatever education Joseph received as a child would have involved memorising Torah (what we now have as the first five books of the Bible). No doubt the shattering news brought Deuteronomy 22:22-27 to mind, which outlined what was to be done in his present context. Only one thought could have filled Joseph's mind: In the absence of any sexual assault, Mary had committed a capital offence. Indeed, her adultery broke the entire second table of the law: it dishonoured her parents; in essence it was like killing Joseph; it was stealing what was pledged to him; she had lied to him; she had desired something that did not belong to her.

In God's providence, Joseph lived in occupied territory under Roman rule. The Jews did not have the authority to enact the death penalty (although sometimes it may have been put into effect by mob rule). But the just thing to do under the circumstances was to treat Mary as guilty and divorce her—an act of public humiliation. It was a nightmare scenario.

But, Joseph thought, *I will try to do it as quietly as possible.*

The combination is significant. It tells us that Joseph was a Micah 6:8 man: he would "do justice ... love kindness and ... walk humbly with ... God." God had surely been preparing him to be the father to whom his own Son could be submissive and in whose home he would later "increase in wisdom and in stature and in favour with God and man" (Luke 2:51-52).

But we mustn't overlook something Matthew says here. Joseph did not act in haste. "He *considered* these things" and apparently, still considering them, he went to bed to sleep on it (Matthew 1:20, my emphasis). The same verb is used in Acts 10:19 of Peter reflecting on the meaning of the vision he received at the house of Simon the Tanner in Joppa. Although the Old Testament law was clear enough, like Peter, Joseph was still trying to work things out in his mind. On the one hand there seemed to be no question of what he should do. And yet... Was there something holding him back?

Joseph usually acted decisively. Later on we learn that he emigrated with less than a day's notice! All he needed to "divorce her quietly" was the presence of two witnesses. Perhaps time would bring healing and acceptance. Yes, that was surely God's way for the righteous man.

So why, as Matthew tells us, is Joseph still trying to work things out when he goes to bed? Because there is something about the conclusion he has reached that doesn't fit. The picture doesn't seem quite right, but he can't see why.

Joseph had fitted a wrong piece into the picture—the conclusion that Mary must have committed adultery. Once the right piece was in place the picture would look entirely different. Yet for now it seems that there was a restraint on his spirit. God was restraining him from acting—at least until the next day—long enough for him to have a dream that would provide the missing piece of the puzzle. And then his waking nightmare would be transformed.

We will learn more about Joseph's dream tomorrow. But for today there is an important practical lesson. Our Bibles are not lists of "do this; don't do that" telling us what to do in every specific situation. It is, therefore, not always equally clear what we should do. To give a common example, how do you know it is God's will for you to marry a particular person when there is no verse in the Bible telling you to do that? Or, for that matter, to take a certain job? Or to move to a particular place? Or to begin a particular ministry?

God guides our lives by teaching us to live according to his will revealed in Scripture. We are to apply its principles and precepts to the circumstances and situations in which we find ourselves.

But if, having done this, we sense a restraint on our spirit—a sense of "something doesn't seem right here, but I am not sure why"—then we would be wise, Joseph-like, to hesitate: to sleep on it until we have more light. Sometimes there is something in the Scriptures we don't fully understand. Or there may be something in our situation that still needs to be clarified before we can take the next step. At such times we need to wait on the Lord and wait for the Lord to unfold his plans.

That's what Joseph seems to have done—thankfully.

How do we do this? I am reminded of the answer given by John Flavel, a minister in Dartmouth, England in the 17th century. He wrote these wise words to guide us when we are uncertain what to do:

1. *Get the true fear of God upon your hearts; be really afraid of offending him …*
2. *Study the word more, and the concerns and interests of the world less …*
3. *Reduce what you know into practice, and you shall know what is your duty to practise …*
   [In other words, work out what you should do in the light of what you already understand of God's will—that is what you should do now!]
4. *Pray for illumination and direction in the way you should go; beg the Lord to guide you in*

> *straits [difficult circumstances], and that he*
> *would not suffer you to fall into sin ...*
> 5. *And this being done, follow providence as far*
>   *as it agrees with the word, and no further.*[2]

Joseph would have liked that!

⌐────────○

> *Oh, thou art greatly to be feared,*
> *Thou art so prompt to bless!*
> *The dread to miss such love as thine*
> *Makes fear but love's excess.*
>
> *But fear is love, and love is fear,*
> *And in and out they move;*
> *But fear is an intenser joy*
> *Than mere unfrightened love.*
>
> *They love thee little, if at all,*
> *Who do not fear thee much;*
> *If love is thine attraction, Lord!*
> *Fear is thy very touch.*
>
> *"The Fear of God"*
> *F.W. Faber (1814-1863)*

⌐────────○

---

2 John Flavel, "The Mystery of Providence" in *The Works of John Flavel* Vol. 4 (1820; reprinted Banner of Truth Trust, 1969), p 470-471.

Lord, thank you for the way you prepared Joseph to be our Saviour's adoptive father. And thank you, too, for the way you shaped and moulded his life to welcome the Lord Jesus. We confess that sometimes, like him, we do not know what to do, or even how to pray. Grant us your wisdom we ask. Amen.

6. DREAM
ANGEL

I have a friend who is an expert in international space law. I pulled his leg when he told me he was involved in an international space commission to discuss the legal status of the first message to come from outer space, should that happen in the future. But then he went on to serve on another commission to determine the legal status of the first extraterrestrial to arrive on Planet Earth!

Do you believe in extraterrestrials? The Bible does, in a way; it calls them "angels." They come here, but they are not *from* here. Heaven, the immediate presence of God, is their home.

During the months before Jesus was born, one such angel, named Gabriel (meaning "God is great"), was kept busy. He visited Zechariah, the father of John the Baptist (Luke 1:19); six months or so later he also visited Mary (1:26). Now an angel—perhaps Gabriel again?—was visiting Joseph. But this time he came "in a dream."

You can't help wondering: why did Joseph's angelic visit take place during a dream? It happened twice more (Matthew 2:13, 19) and perhaps a fourth time too (2:22).

In the Old Testament God sometimes revealed his purposes through dreams. Was the "dream angel visit" meant to reassure Joseph that God was continuing to reveal himself to his people?

Perhaps there is another reason. Remember, Joseph had thought through his response to this nightmare situation the best he could, without taking any action. He had tried to think biblically and act obediently. He went to bed with a troubled mind. He had reached a conclusion—and yet something seemed to be holding him back.

Perhaps you know the experience. You work through an issue or a situation carefully, trying to apply the wisdom of Scripture to it. You think you see what to do. And yet questions linger in your mind, and you feel an inexplicable restraint on your spirit. Something just doesn't seem right. And then light seems to dawn on you, or something happens, and things become clear.

Joseph needed that "something" to happen. And it did. The dream angel gave him the missing piece of the jigsaw puzzle, without which he would have been unable to discern the Lord's will.

God was untangling the knot that Joseph had tried to loosen in his waking hours. He did so in a way that prevented Joseph from thinking he had worked it out for himself. And in his kindness God dissolved any fears Joseph might have in wondering whether he was following his own plans and desires with disregard to God's word.

The child in Mary's womb was not the fruit of her sin but of "the Holy Spirit" (Matthew 1:20). This was the clue Joseph had needed. Now things began to fall into place. He was given light on his situation. As the angel said, he had no need to fear he was disobeying the Lord by marrying Mary! So, no matter what the consequences might be, he would do what the angel said. He did not need any further consideration. Matthew's words wonderfully convey his immediate obedience. "When Joseph woke from sleep ... he took his wife." Now, that's decisiveness!

We should pause for a moment here to think about this dream revelation because it's possible to draw a wrong conclusion from Joseph's experience. Dream revelations are not normal in Scripture; they occur infrequently and almost always in clusters—as here and in chapter 2:12, 13, 19 and 22. (The only other references to dreams in the New Testament are: Matthew 27:19; Acts 2:17; Jude 1:8.)

When events like this are recorded in Scripture, it is normally at a strategic point in God's purposes, when he is acting in a crisis situation in his kingdom or inaugurating a new stage in its advance. That was true here. God was doing something new, and Joseph needed to know it. And the Lord Jesus was going to come under fierce attack by Herod, so Joseph needed to be with Mary to protect him.

So even in the Bible these dream revelations are unusual. Nobody in Scripture receives their regular guidance from dreams (or encounters with angels for that matter). There is no record of Jesus having dream revelations, and angels appeared to him only twice—both times in critical moments for the kingdom of God (Mark 1:13 in the wilderness temptations; Luke 22:43 when he was in Gethsemane). So, we should probably beware of people who claim that God regularly reveals himself to them through dreams or by angel visits.

Yet at the same time the Bible teaches us that angels minister to God's children, and often in ways we never know (Hebrews 1:14, 13:2). But why here? Because Joseph was to be the defender of God's king and kingdom in the coming hour of crisis. And he needed to be sure that he was doing God's will and not just his own.

The truly admirable thing about Joseph was that what he most feared was failing to obey the Lord. He knew how important it is to have "the true fear of God upon your hearts; be really afraid of offending him" long before John Flavel wrote those words. That was why the dream angel said to him, "Joseph, son of David [he had probably never in his life been addressed in that dignified way!], do not fear to take Mary as your wife." *It is the will of your Lord.*

You can't help admiring Joseph. Or, as Matthew wants us to see, you can't help admiring God's work in his life. It was because of the way the Father in heaven had shaped and prepared him that Joseph was ready to be entrusted with the task of being the father on earth for God's incarnate Son. For Joseph was willing to do whatever God said.

Are you?

O love that wilt not let me go,
I rest my weary soul in thee!
I give thee back the life I owe,
That in thine ocean depths its flow
May richer, fuller be.

O joy that seekest me through pain,
I cannot close my heart to thee;
I see the rainbow through the rain,
And feel the promise is not vain,
That morn shall tearless be.

"O Love That Wilt Not Let Me Go"
George Matheson (1842-1906)

Father, you have taught us that the angels, who see your face, are interested in us because they admire their King, who at such cost has won our salvation. Help us therefore, we ask, that we too may grow in wonder and praise at all that your Son has done for us. Amen.

7. "TIDINGS OF COMFORT AND JOY"?

Joseph was, apparently, "afraid to take Mary" as his wife (Matthew 1:20, NIV). Some men are afraid of getting married; they fear permanent commitment. But Joseph's fear was different—and healthier. It was not a fear of marriage but a fear of God—a reluctance to do anything that would grieve him.

The fear of God often seems to be what people fear most of all! Even Christians shiver a little whenever it is mentioned. Yet in the Bible it is a mark of grace—it's the best and healthiest fear you could have. For we are commanded to fear God.

"Well, yes," someone might say, "but that's only the Old Testament." Well, no: it's the New Testament. It is Jesus (Matthew 10:28); it is the first Christians (Acts 9:31); it is Paul (2 Corinthians 7:1); it is the author of Hebrews (Hebrews 12:28); it is Simon Peter (1 Peter 2:17); it is all the saints (Revelation 15:4).

What, then, is this good fear? It is the desire to live under God's smile, and therefore to avoid anything that might cause him to frown. Fearing God means, as our spiritual forefathers said, living *coram Deo*—in the presence of God—because you know that he wants to "bless you and keep you … make his face to shine upon you and … lift up his countenance upon you and give you peace" (Numbers 6:24-26).

Joseph was a righteous man, and, by definition, righteous men fear God. He would rather have experienced pain than sense God's frown. Whatever dark hole he felt he was facing, his fear of the Lord was a fixed point in his life.

But now the angel was telling him not to fear that taking Mary would offend God: *He knows you do not want to grieve him; he knows you can see no option but divorce. But he also knows there is something that doesn't seem to make sense to you. You are right. The Lord has sent me to tell you what it is: Mary's child is not the fruit of her sin but of God's Spirit. Marry her!*

Imagine how Joseph might have felt as he woke up. If he had had access to our hymn books, he would surely have been able to sing:

> *Praise to the Lord,*
> *Who o'er all things so wondrously reigneth,*
> *Shelters thee under his wings,*
> *Yea, so gently sustaineth:*
> *Hast thou not seen*
> *How thy heart's wishes have been*
> *Granted in what he ordaineth?*[3]

---

3 From the hymn "Praise to the Lord, the Almighty, the King of Creation" by Joachim Neander (1650-1680), translated by Catherine Winkworth (1829-1878) and others.

Strictly speaking, Jesus' birth was not supernatural; it was as "natural" as ours. But his conception in the womb of a virgin was supernatural: the work of the Holy Spirit in Mary.

People today often respond, "But we are modern, scientific, 21st-century people, not 1st-century artisans! We know that virgin conceptions don't happen!"

Joseph knew that just as well as we do. But he knew something else. From his childhood he had heard and memorised the majestic opening words of the Scroll of Genesis. In the darkness God had created the heavens and the earth (Genesis 1:1). When there were no spectators, he had brought the world into existence out of nothing. It was therefore not beyond his power to work in the darkness of the womb of a young virgin without the help of man, and to bring a child into the world.

Joseph believed this. Yet it must have been overwhelming to learn that God was exercising that power now and that he was doing it in the life of the young woman Joseph had intended to marry.

How much did Joseph understand about what was happening here? Did he see that God was doing something radically new, and yet accomplishing it from within our humanity? Did he sense that this must be the start of the new creation, which God had promised through the prophets?

Do you ever wonder how you would have reacted? Perhaps you're thankful you were not in Joseph's shoes!

But there is an important sense in which we do share his shoes.

Joseph was challenged to believe that God had done this. So are we.

Joseph was challenged to welcome Jesus the Saviour. So are we.

Joseph was challenged to devote the rest of his life to Jesus. So are we.

Are you willing... or not?

That decision is always a costly one. Joseph's experience illustrates a broader biblical principle: welcoming Christ into your life means that you will share in what happened to Jesus. Jesus himself taught that: "Because you are not of the world, but I chose you out of the world, therefore the world hates you" (John 15:19). Paul experienced it, as he tells us in various places in his letters (2 Corinthians 4:10-12 being one of the most dramatic).

At first sight, as we read on in these two chapters in Matthew, it looks as though where Joseph goes, Jesus goes. But it is really the other way round, isn't it? Where Jesus goes, Joseph also goes. If Jesus has to become a refugee in Egypt, so does Joseph. If Jesus has to be brought up in Nazareth, to Nazareth Joseph must go.

So what we see in Joseph's life is a striking illustration of a permanent principle: the Christ we receive by faith is also the Christ who shapes our life of faith. And those who come to believe in him discover, like Joseph and Peter and Paul, that life takes on a "Jesus shape." Thus we who live are "always carrying around in the body the death of Jesus, so that the life of Jesus may also be manifested in our bodies" (2 Corinthians 4:10).

This is the way in which we are being transformed into his likeness.

Joseph must have known that welcoming Christ would be costly. And we need to know that too.

But he is worth it all, isn't he?

———

How silently, how silently,
The wondrous gift is given.
So God imparts to human hearts
The blessings of his heaven.
No ear may hear his coming,
But in this world of sin,
Where meek souls will receive him
Still the dear Christ enters in.

"O Little Town of Bethlehem"
Phillips Brooks (1835-1893)

———

Lord Jesus, the challenge of receiving you and living for you can be overwhelming at times. But we want to be yours, to trust you, to love you, to serve you. And we thank you that when we are yours, you make us more and more like yourself. Amen.

8. WHAT'S IN A NAME?

New parents are sometimes in emotional agonies over choosing their baby's name. It all seems so permanent.

I once immensely enjoyed a conversation with a psychiatrist who had a practice on London's famous Harley Street (we were speaking at the same conference!). He told me the story behind his Christian name, which was Gaius. He had been brought up in Welsh Pentecostalism. When he was born, his mother told his elder brother, "Go to 'the prophet' and ask him what the name of your new brother should be."

The boy came back with the cryptic answer "John, three, one." Slightly puzzled, his mother thought, "Surely I am not to call my baby 'Nicodemus'!" (who is mentioned in John 3:1). "Go back to the prophet," she said, "and ask him, 'Are you sure he's to be called 'Nicodemus'?" The brother soon returned, but chastened. "Sorry, mum," he said. "The prophet says, 'It's not John, three, one but *three, John, one.*'" And so "Nicodemus" became "Gaius" (to whom John's third letter was written)!

Every child's name has a story behind it that gives it special significance—even if not always as quirky as this one!

That was just as true in Jesus' day. The very fact that Matthew begins with a lengthy genealogy tells us how much family tradition meant to a 1st-century Jew. Luke tells us that there was great consternation among the relatives and neighbours of Zechariah and Elizabeth (not to mention the family pressure!) when she insisted her son's name was John: "None of your relatives is called by that name," they objected (Luke 1:61). *How could you slight family tradition like this?* But it was the name the angel of the Lord had told John's parents to give him.

Now Matthew tells us that an angel brought a similar message to Joseph: God had chosen the name of Mary's son—Jesus. There is no "Jesus" in the genealogy of Matthew 1:1-17! At a stretch, perhaps, friends might have wondered if the name was chosen because of Joseph's admiration for Joshua. But the angel gave the real explanation: "He shall save his people from their sins" (Matthew 1:21). Yeshua (Joshua/Jesus) means "Yahweh [the LORD] saves."

In the Old Testament, Joshua had been God's instrument in bringing his people into the land of promise. That was always the end in view in their "salvation" from Egypt. But where Mary's son was concerned, the name expressed something deeper: Jesus himself was the God who saves.

Perhaps the angel's words would have reminded Joseph of the closing verses of Psalm 130: "With the Lord there is steadfast love, and with him is plentiful redemption. *And he will redeem Israel from all his iniquities*" (Psalm 130:7-8, my emphasis).

Steadfast love and plentiful redemption from all iniquities—how would these words be fulfilled in and through the child Mary was now carrying?

Joseph knew the basic plot line of the Bible—the gradual unfolding of the promise of Genesis 3:15, which said that a Redeemer would come from the seed of the woman and crush the head of the serpent.

God had spoken these words as a judgment curse on the serpent, but Eve held on to them as a promise of salvation. Later, when her first son was born, she cried, "I have gotten a man with the help of the Lord" (4:1). But her son Cain was not the Redeemer Eve was hoping for. Far from crushing the serpent, he bludgeoned his own brother to death in a field.

Later, Lamech entertained a similar hope for his son. He "called his name Noah, saying, 'Out of the ground that the Lord has cursed this one shall bring us relief from our work and from the painful toil of our hands'" (5:29).

The name "Noah" sounds like the Hebrew word for rest. Noah was not the promised Deliverer who would bring rest. But elements in his life—the way he went through the judgment of God in the ark, which eventually came to rest on dry land—served as a picture, a pointer to the one who says about himself, "Come to me … and *I will give you rest* … and you will find rest for your souls" (Matthew 11:28-29).

Perhaps Joseph was reminded of another passage about God's promised salvation. Isaiah had spoken about a coming Servant of the Lord who would be "wounded for our transgressions" and "crushed for our iniquities" (Isaiah 53:5).

Joseph's contemporaries hoped for a Messiah who would be a military conqueror, delivering them from Roman thraldom and leading them into the glorious new age promised by the prophets. But Joseph was learning that Mary's child would fulfil the ancient prophecies in a different way. He would deal with an older and more destructive enemy than Rome. For the people's greatest needs—then as now—were not sociopolitical; they were spiritual and moral. The child's name was to be Jesus because he would "save his people *from their sins*" (Matthew 1:21, my emphasis).

Did Joseph realise that the "people" this child would save would not only be Jews? Soon Joseph would meet a group of Gentile scholars from the east who were searching for the newborn king who might be the Messiah. They were an early indication that the people Jesus was going to save were "from every tribe and language and people and nation" (Revelation 5:9).

We sometimes ask, "What's in a name?" In the case of this name, Jesus, the Christian's answer is "Everything". Because "Jesus" is not only a name; it is who he is. He is the same today as he was to Simon Peter, and to Zacchaeus and to Bartimaeus, and to Mary and Martha. For our "Jesus ... is the same yesterday and today and for ever" (Hebrews 13:8). Think of that this Christmas; he will never stop being Jesus—the Saviour. And, as Paul says, "Whatever you do, in word or deed, do everything in the name of the Lord Jesus, giving thanks to God the Father through him" (Colossians 3:17).

All hail the power of Jesus' name!
Let angels prostrate fall;
Bring forth the royal diadem
To crown him Lord of all.

Ye seed of Israel's chosen race,
Ye ransomed from the fall,
Hail him who saves you by his grace,
And crown him Lord of all.

Ye Gentile sinners, ne'er forget
The wormwood and the gall;
Go spread your trophies at his feet,
And crown him Lord of all.

O that with yonder sacred throng
We at his feet may fall,
Join in the everlasting song
And crown him Lord of all!

"All Hail the Power of Jesus' Name"
Edward Perronet (1752-1792)
Altered by John Rippon (1751-1836)

Our Father, you have taught us in your word that this Child, once lowly born and crucified, is now at your right hand, and that one day every knee will bow at the name of Jesus. Thank you so much that although now exalted, he is still the same Jesus. Amen.

9. "ISAIAH HATH FORETOLD HIM"

Once, when I was at school, one of my closest friends stood up at the morning assembly and announced: "The Scripture reading today comes from the Gospel according to Isaiah." "Oh no!" I thought, "He's going to be so embarrassed; Isaiah isn't a Gospel!"

But in one sense he had spoken the truth. Isaiah isn't technically a Gospel, but it does contain good news, which is what the word means. Perhaps that explains why the New Testament contains more quotations from Isaiah than from any other book. Matthew's Gospel alone has as many as 40 of them. You can imagine Matthew "joining up" the dots he found in Isaiah and seeing an outline of the life and work of the Lord Jesus.

Here, in Matthew 1:22-23, Matthew quotes Isaiah 7:14:

All this took place to fulfil what the Lord had spoken by the prophet:
"Behold, the virgin shall conceive and bear a son, and they shall call his name Immanuel."

At a time of national crisis, God sent Isaiah to Ahaz the king of Israel, telling him to ask for a sign. Ahaz replied very piously, "I will not ask, and I will not put the LORD to the test," but in fact he was a man who wanted to do things his way rather than God's. Isaiah responded that if that were the case, God himself would send a sign: "Behold, the virgin shall conceive and bear a son, and shall call his name Immanuel" (Isaiah 7:10-14).

But in Ahaz's case, this "sign" was not pointing to good things. The word that came to Ahaz was that his royal house was doomed: "Before the boy knows how to refuse the evil and choose the good ... the LORD will bring upon you [Ahaz] and upon your people and upon your father's house such days as have not come since the day that Ephraim departed from Judah—the king of Assyria" (7:16-17).

Isaiah goes on to talk about a time of judgment and destruction, and about the birth of his own son, whom God commanded him to name Maher-shalal-hash-baz ("The spoil speeds, the prey hurries", 8:1-5). But after a time of darkness, then, eventually, would come a time of light—brought about by the birth of a child who would be called "Wonderful Counsellor, Mighty God, Everlasting Father, Prince of Peace" (9:6).

Isaiah could have had no idea of the total time span envisaged in these divinely given insights. Only when prophecies are fulfilled are they explained. Until then there is always something veiled. Whatever immediate reference Isaiah's prophecy may have had, Matthew saw that it perfectly described the events surrounding the birth of Jesus. In him Isaiah's prophecy was filled out to the full.

In Matthew 4:15-16 Matthew refers to Isaiah 9:1-7, identifying Jesus as the "great light" that would dawn on those in darkness: the son whose kingdom would last forever. He would be the "shoot from the stump of Jesse" on whom "the Spirit of the Lord shall rest" (Isaiah 11:1-9), who would bring cosmic restoration. He would be the servant of the Lord who would "not cry aloud or lift up his voice, or make it heard in the street; a bruised reed he will not break, and a faintly burning wick he will not quench" (42:1-3). Jesus would be the light to the nations (49:6), the one who had "the tongue of those who are taught," who would "know how to sustain with a word him who is weary" (50:4). And supremely he would be the one "despised and rejected by men; a man of sorrows, and acquainted with grief" but who would be "wounded for our transgressions" (53:3-5).

The son to be born of a virgin slowly emerges from the shadows in Isaiah's later prophecies, and steps out into the full light of day as the Suffering Servant who would "save his people from their sins." All this Matthew could see in hindsight because he had come to know the Lord Jesus. He saw the reality that was still obscure to Isaiah.

Young virgins had gone on to conceive and bear sons throughout the ages. It happens all the time. But Matthew saw in Jesus a unique "filling full" of Isaiah's words: his conception took place when his mother *was still a virgin!*

Matthew tells us that this child was to have two names: "Jesus," indicating *what he came to accomplish* (through him God would save his people) and "Immanuel," indicating *who he was* (God himself with his people). The virgin conception and birth of Jesus was the assurance to Mary and Joseph that the child was himself Immanuel.

And before we say, "But I can't work out how a virgin conception could possibly happen," we should remember that we can't actually "work out" how God makes anything "happen"! How did he create all things out of nothing? Or part the Red Sea? Or raise Jesus from the dead? We would need to be God himself to be able to "work out" all he does! Christianity is a supernatural faith from start to finish, and the virgin conception is but one element in it.

Matthew's point is that this unique event is nothing less than a new creation. The words "genealogy" (in Matthew 1:1) and "birth" (in verse 18) both translate the same Greek word—*genesis*. God was beginning again in Jesus Christ.

There is another important lesson that the virgin conception teaches us. God brings it about, not man. Joseph did nothing. Yet God also works *in our humanity*—Jesus didn't drop down into the manger from heaven, but was conceived by Mary. But she was passive, not active. She couldn't conceive the Saviour on her own.

The message? From beginning to end, it is God who saves; we cannot save ourselves. God sets us to one side here, in order to bring us to his side in Jesus Christ. Yet how easy that is to forget amid all the hustle and bustle of the Christmas season, as we race to get a hundred and one good deeds done before the big day. We do well to remember the words of Archbishop William Temple: "All is of God; the only thing of my very own which I can contribute to my own redemption is the sin from which I need to be redeemed."[4]

That is what Christmas is really all about.

Lo, how a rose e'er blooming
From tender stem hath sprung!
Of Jesse's lineage coming
As men of old have sung.
It came, a flower bright,
Amid the cold of winter
When half spent was the night.

This flower, whose fragrance tender
With sweetness fills the air,
Dispels with glorious splendour
The darkness everywhere.
True man, yet very God
From sin and death He saves us
And lightens every load.

"Lo, How a Rose E'er Blooming"
Traditional
Translated by Theodore Baker (1851-1934)

---

4 William Temple, *Nature, Man and God* (MacMillan and Co, 1934), p 401.

Father, forgive us if we ever imagined we could save ourselves. Thank you for keeping your promises to send your Son to be our Saviour. We thank you that he is Immanuel—God with us—as well as being our Wonderful Counsellor, our Prince of Peace, and the Suffering Servant who died for our sins. Amen.

10. THE WAY OF OBEDIENCE

Has the prospect of doing the right thing ever given you cause to be afraid? For Joseph, it had—at least at first.

Joseph's experience of angelic revelation was quite different from Mary's. It wasn't only that the angel appeared to Mary when she was awake but came to Joseph when he was asleep. Mary was told about the conception of Jesus *before* it took place (Luke 1:31); but Joseph learned of it only *after* it had already happened. Why did the word of the Lord come to them in these two different ways and at two different times?

One reason is, obviously, that Mary needed to know in advance; Joseph didn't. Perhaps another is that Joseph needed to be tested to prepare him for the trials that lay ahead.

It might seem from the angelic messages that the young couple did have one thing in common: they were both told not to be afraid (Matthew 1:20; Luke 1:30). But their fears were different. Mary was afraid because she had just encountered the angel Gabriel. Joseph's encounter was much less fearful—after all, he was dreaming. In his case the angel had come to help him deal with a two-stage fear: on the one hand, the fear of grieving God by following the desires of his own heart, and then, on the other, the fear of the consequences that might flow from marrying Mary.

If Joseph went ahead with his marriage to Mary, the child she was carrying would be born only a few months afterwards. Everyone would know. And where was Mary now anyway? She had probably already left home and gone to her cousin Elizabeth. (Incidentally, what a wonderful family circle God had given her.) There was no opportunity to discuss with her what they would do. How could he discuss it with anybody? Who could give him wise counsel?

But the angel's message was *Continue to trust the Lord, Joseph. You never need to be afraid of doing God's will.*

Little did Joseph know what God had planned! For some months later he and Mary would begin an extended period away from home, conveniently far away from prying eyes and loose tongues:

> *In those days a decree went out from Caesar*
> *Augustus that all the world should be registered …*
> *And all went to be registered, each to his own*
> *town. And Joseph also went up from Galilee, from*
> *the town of Nazareth, to Judea, to the city of*
> *David which is called Bethlehem, because he was*
> *of the house and lineage of David, to be registered*

> *with Mary, his betrothed, who was with child.*
> *And while they were there, the time came for her*
> *to give birth. (Luke 2:1-6)*

Nor would Joseph have been able to imagine that strangers from the east would bring them valuable gifts, or that they would then be refugees in Egypt—yet well supplied with these gifts to sustain them in exile.

Our God is not what is sometimes called a *deus ex machina*—a divine figure in a play, appearing as if by magic to sort out the mess. He does not pop in and out of history as occasion demands. Matthew 1:1-17 has already underlined that he is Lord of every detail of it. Now Joseph was about to discover that for himself. He did not need to fear. The heavenly Father was in total control.

This is every Christian's security too, as the Heidelberg Catechism, a 16th-century statement of faith, famously says:

> *Question:*
> *What is your only comfort in life and in death?*
>
> *Answer:*
> *That I am not my own, but belong—*
> *body and soul, in life and in death—*
> *to my faithful Saviour, Jesus Christ.*
> *He has fully paid for all my sins with his*
> *precious blood,*
> *and has delivered me from the tyranny of*
> *the devil.*

> *He also watches over me in such a way*
> *that not a hair can fall from my head*
> *without the will of my Father in heaven;*
> *in fact, all things must work together for my*
> *salvation.*
> *Because I belong to him,*
> *Christ, by his Holy Spirit,*
> *also assures me of eternal life*
> *and makes me wholeheartedly willing and ready*
> *from now on to live for him.*

To us, Joseph seems a silent man. He appears only once in the Gospel records outside of the birth narratives in Matthew and Luke; he never speaks. We know nothing more about him. But he is a wonderful illustration of the principle articulated by the slave-ship-captain-turned-hymn-writer John Newton:

> *'Twas grace that taught my heart to fear,*
> *And grace my fears relieved.*

And so, when Joseph woke up, "he did as the angel of the Lord commanded him; he took his wife" (Matthew 1:24).

We can't help admiring Joseph. He heard the word of God; he believed the word of God; and he obeyed the word of God, whatever the cost might be.

Christmas Eve services beyond number have begun with the singing of Cecil Francis Alexander's carol "Once in Royal David's City." Every year we hear these words:

And through all his wondrous childhood
He would honour and obey,
Love and watch the lowly maiden
In whose gentle arms he lay…

But Jesus must have watched Joseph too.

If you think about this, it may make you hold your breath in wonder for a moment: Joseph was the man God chose and prepared to protect and nurture his incarnate Son. Eventually, as the Lord Jesus grew older, he must have spent more time with him than he did with Mary. Yes, he loved his mother to the end; but he also loved the lowly carpenter into whose care his heavenly Father had entrusted him. He must have watched him for hours in the workshop and worked with him on his projects. From his lips he would have heard the psalms of David and the ancient stories of grace. He would have heard the prophecies that foretold his death. And perhaps from Joseph, too, he heard the words of Isaiah: "This is the one to whom I will look: he who is humble and contrite in spirit, and trembles at my word" (Isaiah 66:2).

When we walk with the Lord
In the light of his Word,
What a glory he sheds on our way!
While we do his good will,
He abides with us still,
And with all who will trust and obey.

But we never can prove
The delights of his love
Until all on the altar we lay;
For the favour he shows,
And the joy he bestows,
Are for them who will trust and obey.

Trust and obey, for there's no other way
To be happy in Jesus, but to trust and obey.

"Trust and Obey"
John Henry Sammis (1846-1919)

Lord, reassure us today that we have nothing to fear if we live in your presence and do your will. You have promised never to leave us and never to forsake us. Give us all the help we will need today to be obedient to your word. Amen.

11. JOSEPH'S RESTRAINT

When Joseph awoke from his dream, "he did as the angel of the Lord commanded him: he took his wife" (Matthew 1:24). Now they were living together as husband and wife. Yet, says Matthew, Joseph "knew her not until she had given birth to a son" (v 25).

Why would a modern Bible translation like the English Standard Version continue to use such archaic-sounding language? We all know what it means. But what we would say is *Joseph abstained from sexual relations with Mary until after Jesus was born.* So is Victorian prudery still alive among Bible translators?

On the contrary: "Joseph ... knew her not" translates what Matthew wrote. And his simple statement has a good deal to teach us.

Matthew's language echoes words from the beginning of the Bible's story: "Adam knew Eve his wife" (Genesis 4:1, 25). The physical relations between a man and a woman are intended in part to be an expression of the unreserved, deep, and lifelong self-surrendering of two people to each other. They are a physical way of communicating our total devotion and lifelong commitment. In them, we are saying, "I am yours, and all that I am is yours, without reservation."

Without that, sexual relations are a mere satisfaction of our own desires. They become a kind of hypocrisy in which we physically express something we don't really mean. That is why God reserves them for married life.

All this we can learn from the verb "knew". But in fact what Matthew tells us is that "Joseph … *knew [Mary] not* until she had given birth to her son."

Matthew offers no explanation. But it is not hard to guess: in this way they were confirming the message of the angel. It was their seal on God's act, and their testimony to each other that they believed what God had said. And it also tells us that Joseph—and Mary too, we must not forget—had a higher goal in life than fulfilling their own natural desires. God had prepared them well for each other—and for the Lord Jesus.

There are some unexpected, but important, lessons for us here.

One is that the restraint of our good and God-given natural desires is not in itself harmful. True, that principle can become twisted. God "richly provides us with everything to enjoy" (1 Timothy 6:17); but our instinct needs to be "What is the wise thing to do, and what will tend most to God's glory?" In a number of situations—including if we are unmarried—biblically regulated abstinence is both wise and for God's glory. And if times like Christmas feel more difficult for us partly because we are single, remember that it carries a hidden message for us. The Saviour who came at Christmas was truly human; but he too was single. No one understands our longing for companionship more fully than he does. And no one can help us offer our singleness to God better than he can.

There is another lesson here, perhaps a less obvious one. There was nothing wrong with Mary and Joseph having normal sexual relations. They were married. But "there's nothing wrong with it" was never the principle on which they acted.

Saying "There's nothing wrong with it, so we're doing it" was one reason why Paul described the Corinthians as "people of the flesh ... infants in Christ" and not "spiritual people" (1 Corinthians 3:1).

"All things are lawful for me" (in other words, *There's nothing wrong with it, so we're doing it,* 6:12) had become a mantra among some of the Corinthian Christians. Paul responds by teaching them that "There's nothing wrong with it!" is not the principle by which Christians live. True, "Is there anything wrong with it?" can serve as a boundary marker; if something is wrong, the Christian avoids it. But it's not the whole story. There are additional questions we need to ask if we are to live wisely and for God's glory.

Here are four questions Paul taught the Corinthians to ask when evaluating their choices. These apply to anything from the food we eat and the way we spend our money to the television we watch and the relationships we pursue.

First, *is it helpful?* "'All things are lawful for me,' but not all things are helpful" (6:12). We need to consider, "Is this really helpful—to others, or to myself?" If I am reluctant to ask this, then there is something wrong. I am behaving as a spiritual "infant"—like a pouting child complaining that "there's nothing wrong with it," and so they will please themselves.

Remember, too, that growing in grace is never merely a matter of negative avoidance but also of positive Christlikeness. Jesus "went about doing good" (Acts 10:38), not simply avoiding what was wrong!

Second, *will it enslave me?* "'All things are lawful for me,' but I will not be dominated by anything" (1 Corinthians 6:12). Many things can be "more-ish". They differ from person to person. They may be perfectly legitimate, but *in our case* they become easily dominant. We should not allow ourselves to be enslaved by anything, however good. Insisting that "all things are lawful" may turn out to be an indication of my bondage.

Third, *how will it affect others?* "Take care that this right of yours does not somehow become a stumbling block to the weak" (8:9). The Corinthians faced a question few of us will encounter: should a believer eat meat that had been offered to an idol? Paul knew that "an idol has no real existence" (8:4). A good steak is a good steak! We are at liberty to eat it. But that is not the only issue. Paul raises another: *Will my eating this meat cause someone to stumble?* My exercising my liberty may become a brother's or sister's downfall. If so, I will abstain. After all, "Food will not commend us to God.

We are no worse off if we do not eat, and no better off if we do" (8:8).

If I insist on exercising my Christian liberty—or worse, flaunt it—I am in danger of being in bondage to it. And if I insist on flaunting my liberty in the face of "weaker" brothers and sisters, I certainly am enslaved by it. It's not the mark of maturity that I pretend it to be but the reverse.

Fourth, *does it edify?* "'All things are lawful,' but not all things build up. Let no one seek his own good, but the good of his neighbour" (10:23-24). Paul gives us a simple guideline: How are my actions going to build up, strengthen, and bless my fellow believers and the church family? Am I loving my neighbour as myself, or only loving myself? Is what I want to do more important than what will build up someone else? "Let each of us please his neighbour for his good, to build him up," says Paul elsewhere. "For Christ did not please himself" (Romans 15:2-3).

Joseph and Mary had already learned that there are more important considerations if we want to glorify God than "There's nothing wrong with it!" For them, as for us, the most important question of all is: how can we live wisely, for the glory of God and for the blessing of others?

And with this comes wonderful blessing for ourselves. I was taught as a child that joy is spelt Jesus first, Others next, and Yourself last. If you want to experience true joy this Christmas, then that's the place to start.

Sacred infant all divine
What a tender love was thine
Thus to come from highest bliss,
Down to such a world as this!

Teach, O teach us, holy Child,
By thy face so meek and mild,
Teach us to resemble thee,
In thy sweet humility.

"See Amid the Winter's Snow"
Edward Caswell (1814-1878)

Lord Jesus Christ, you did not please yourself but lived for your Father's glory and for our blessing. By the same Spirit through whose ministry you entered our human nature, and in whose power you went about doing good, transform us a little more today into your likeness. Amen.

PART 3

THE VISITORS

¹Now after Jesus was born in Bethlehem of Judea in the days of Herod the king, behold, wise men from the east came to Jerusalem, ²saying, "Where is he who has been born king of the Jews? For we saw his star when it rose and have come to worship him." ³When Herod the king heard this, he was troubled, and all Jerusalem with him; ⁴and assembling all the chief priests and scribes of the people, he inquired of them where the Christ was to be born. ⁵They told him, "In Bethlehem of Judea, for so it is written by the prophet:

⁶"'And you, O Bethlehem, in the land of
    Judah,
    are by no means least among the rulers of
    Judah;
    for from you shall come a ruler
    who will shepherd my people Israel.'"

⁷Then Herod summoned the wise men secretly and ascertained from them what time the star had appeared. ⁸And he sent them to Bethlehem, saying, "Go and search diligently for the child, and when you have found him, bring me word, that I too may come

and worship him." ⁹ After listening to the king, they went on their way. And behold, the star that they had seen when it rose went before them until it came to rest over the place where the child was. ¹⁰ When they saw the star, they rejoiced exceedingly with great joy. ¹¹ And going into the house, they saw the child with Mary his mother, and they fell down and worshiped him. Then, opening their treasures, they offered him gifts, gold and frankincense and myrrh. ¹² And being warned in a dream not to return to Herod, they departed to their own country by another way.

12. WISE MEN FROM THE EAST

Without warning, Matthew has suddenly transported us to a scene hundreds of miles away from Joseph and Mary! Now we are watching a group of wise men whose adventurous story still captures our imagination. Bethlehem shepherds by comparison were two a penny; the church has never shown any real interest in their names. (They were probably despised in their own day too!) But in the Christian tradition, the wise men have become three in number, have turned into kings, and have even been given names: Caspar, Balthasar, and Melchior. But who were they, really?

They were *magoi*, traditionally translated as "wise men." They were scholars—ancient philosophers. They were the pre-scientific "scientists" of antiquity, observing the cosmos and keeping meticulous records of what they saw. Part of what drove their interest was the conviction that events in the natural order influenced human life. They believed that the heavenly world above them disclosed significant truths about the shape of history around them.

These specific scholars were astronomers who dabbled in what we think of as astrology. Lest we think them primitive by comparison with our sophisticated modern society, we should note that the popular press is much happier to give space to a daily horoscope than it is to give space to a daily Bible exposition. That can only be for one reason: that's what people want!

These scholars had observed a "star" which they had not noticed before—it had to be carrying a special message! Their research, perhaps in the great libraries of the ancient Near-East, led them to the conclusion that a special king of the Jews had been born. They decided they would find him and worship him.

Before we follow their journey, it's worth reflecting on some questions: How did they know that a king of the Jews had been born? And why did they go to *worship* him? What possessed them to make the wearisome journey? How did this "star" make such an impact on their lives?

The Hebrew Bible may have given them clues. This does not necessarily mean they possessed the ancient scrolls (although they might well have done). But some parts of the Bible story would have been known in the east because God's people had been exiled there.

From their ancient records, therefore, the wise men may have known about the pagan prophet Balaam (he with the speaking donkey in Numbers 22!). He came from Pethor, in the region where, centuries later, Nebuchadnezzar defeated the Egyptians at the Battle of Carchemish. Balaam was summoned by Balak, the king of Moab, to pronounce a curse on Israel. Instead he prophesied:

> *I see him, but not now;*
> *I behold him, but not near:*
> *A star shall come out of Jacob,*
> *and a sceptre shall arise out of Israel.*
>
> *(Numbers 24:17)*

Here was a pagan prophecy about a "star" somehow related to the Jewish people ("Jacob"), which predicted a new king ("sceptre"). Perhaps the story of Balaam was still remembered in the traditions of the wise in the ancient Near-East. And now, in the night sky, there was a new "star."

There is another biblical story these scholars may well have known. Centuries after Balaam, a teenager named Daniel had been exiled to Babylon. Re-educated by Nebuchadnezzar's wise men, Daniel had become the wisest of them all. He had explained dreams about a coming king and his kingdom, and also had a stunning vision about a Son of Man who would establish the kingdom of the Most High God, the Ancient of Days (Daniel 2; 4; 7:13-28).

Could it be that these men were wise enough to put two and two together? Even so, this alone would not fully explain their actions. The journey would be long and expensive; interpretations of celestial signs had sometimes proved to be mistaken. Plus the quest for a king might prove dangerous—which indeed it did.

Yet *something* compelled them. Or *someone*. They experienced what the French theologian John Calvin often called "a secret instinct of the Spirit." Every journey to Christ does. Knowing parts of the Bible is one thing; responding to them is another.

Your journey to Christ may not have been so dramatic. You saw no star; instead, by various means, the Spirit drew you to seek and find the Saviour while others didn't.

Some of us, when we look back on our own experience of a "secret instinct of the Spirit," *do* see events and experiences that are remarkable to us. A much-admired Christian friend tells of meeting a man—also in the east—who was "by trade" a passport forger! He purchased stolen passports and reworked them. The photograph of a young woman in one stolen document fascinated him. He felt an inexplicable but irresistible compulsion to find her—which, since he had her passport, he was able to do. Long story short, he met her. Eventually he told her he had fallen in love with her!

Can you imagine the impact of her response? "No, you have not fallen in love with *me*. You have seen Jesus in me, and he has been calling you to himself." It was true, and the one-time passport forger came to faith in Christ!

My story is not so dramatic and unusual. But looking back I can see how God created a "secret instinct" in me through people I met, things that were said, and "happenstances" that took place which, eventually, brought me to Christ. And these are no less remarkable.

So today, in light of the journey of the wise men, take a moment to trace your own journey, and to give thanks for the people and events that combined to bring you to worship Christ. And perhaps you should not be surprised if today you meet someone who, without realising what is happening to them, is experiencing a "secret instinct of the Spirit." Be ready to help them on the road to Christ.

As you do this, I suspect you will find yourself agreeing with the hymn writer William Cowper: God still "moves in a mysterious way his wonders to perform."

⌐————⌐

Come then, let us hasten yonder;
Here let all, great and small,
Kneel in awe and wonder.
Love him who with love is yearning;
Hail the Star that from far
Bright with hope is burning.

"All My Heart This Night Rejoices"
Paul Gerhardt (1607-1676), translated by
Catherine Winkworth (1829-1878)

⌐————⌐

Father, looking back, we can see your hand at work in our lives. You brought some of us to Christ through sorrow and others of us through joy. Thank you for those who pointed us to the Lord Jesus and prayed we would journey towards him. Help us to do the same for others. Amen.

13. A DANGEROUS TURNING

Sometimes we seek God's will, and make wise and good decisions, but then we stumble off the path and end up in what John Bunyan called "By-Path Meadow" or even in "Doubting Castle," face to face with "Giant Despair."[5] Sometimes we do this by thinking that, since we have seen God's big purpose for our lives, we can guess what will happen next. And then we run ahead of God. Perhaps we think, "If the Lord has led me to do this... then it obviously means that this will happen, so I am going to decide to do it..." We end up in a cul-de-sac.

The wise men were neither Christians nor Jewish believers. Yet God had led them through their interest in heavenly signs to make this momentous journey to seek out the new king. They certainly believed they were being led by whatever powers that be. What they did not yet know was that it was the God of the Hebrew Scriptures who was guiding them.

---

5 These are all references to John Bunyan's classic allegory of the Christian life in his book, *The Pilgrim's Progress*.

But there was something they still lacked. They had read the heavens and seen a new star. They perhaps knew traditional prophecies from the annals of their wise men, including the stories of the two prophets Balaam and Daniel, who had both spoken of a coming king. And they had not been able to shake off the urge to find him.

Matthew has already given us a hint that the star the magi saw was heading towards the little town of Bethlehem (Matthew 2:1). Its destination was not the capital city and the palace of Herod the Great. But now, instead of continuing their journey, the magi stopped in Jerusalem. Humanly speaking that was sensible enough; the capital city was, surely, the only place in which an heir to the throne could have been born. Perhaps they assumed that virtually anyone they met on the street could answer their question: "Where is he who has been born king of the Jews? For we saw his star when it rose and have come to worship him" (v 1-2).

It must have been more than a little disconcerting to be met with blank stares! *King? Born recently? A star? You've come from where? How far away is that? Whatever possessed you?! We haven't had a new king born here for ages. The present one must be about 70 years old!*

The present king then was Herod the Great, also known as Herod the Vicious. Perhaps, like the Tudor queen Elizabeth I of England, he had spies everywhere. He heard soon enough about the foreign scholars who were enquiring about a new "king of the Jews." And they were saying they had come "to worship him"! No wonder, when word reached the palace, that Herod "was troubled" (v 3). And whenever Herod's throne shook, Jerusalem shuddered in the aftershock. Everyone knew how vicious he could be. If there really was a new king, his death warrant had already been signed—and probably the death warrants of others too. The citizens of Jerusalem were right to be troubled along with him (v 3).

The story could so easily have ended there. The moment when the wise men's eyes turned earthwards and they began to work things out for themselves was the moment when they endangered their whole pilgrimage. It had not been dependent on their wisdom but on God's. Without further divine intervention and protection, the lives of the new king and his parents, and probably of the wise men themselves, were forfeit. This was almost certainly not the reception these magi were anticipating. But it reminds us that God so often works in ways we don't expect.

Human wisdom had said to these scholars, *If you see a new star, and the scholarly tradition tells you it means a very important new king has been born, then logic tells you that you will find him in a royal palace.*

But *divine wisdom* operates with different presuppositions and on different principles. Given humanity's fallen and sinful condition, God's work of salvation must descend to the least and lowest in order to restore us to God. As the church's Early Fathers saw, the Son of God needed to become what he was not in order that we might become what we are not. God's long-promised

King was therefore born into poverty, not into riches; in humility, not pomp; and in an artisan family, not in a king's palace.

Paul understood this wisdom: "You know the grace of our Lord Jesus Christ, that though he was rich, yet for your sake he became poor, so that by his poverty you might become rich" (2 Corinthians 8:9); "Though he was in the form of God ... [he] emptied himself, by taking the form of a servant, being born in the likeness of men. And being found in human form, he humbled himself by becoming obedient to the point of death, even death on a cross" (Philippians 2: 6-8).

The wooden manger, and now whatever humble house Joseph and Mary had found, was just the beginning of things. Divine wisdom dictated that the Saviour-King would be born into poverty and would live in borrowed accommodation with nowhere of his own to lay his head. And at the end of his life, he would be laid again on wood, this time not in a manger but on a cross, and in his death be accommodated in a borrowed tomb.

This is "the king of the Jews." And he is beyond the imagining of human wisdom. Whether the wise men's misstep was born of ignorance or folly, thankfully—as he often does when we err—God rescued them. He was determined that his plan would not be undermined by human frailty and failure, whether that of wise men losing their way or of a vicious ruler seeking to rid the earth of the knowledge of King Jesus. And his plans will not be derailed by our missteps either, no matter how badly we might have messed up. What wonderful assurance to those of us who feel as though we're limping towards the end of another year, conscious of the erratic footprints we have left behind us.

At the heart of the wisdom of God lies the humility and humiliation of the Lord Jesus. The wise men did not yet understand this. They had not yet reached the place, physically or spiritually, where they would see the wisdom of God in Jesus Christ. Saul of Tarsus made the same mistake. He once thought the message of the cross was weakness and folly—as do most people around us today. But like the wise men, and even more fully and clearly than they did, Saul discovered that Christ incarnate, humbled and crucified, is both the power of God and the wisdom of God (1 Corinthians 1:18-25).

Come, thou Fount of every blessing,
Tune my heart to sing thy grace;
Streams of mercy, never ceasing,
Call for songs of loudest praise.

Prone to wander, Lord, I feel it,
Prone to leave the God I love;
Take my heart, O take and seal it,
Seal it from thy courts above.

"Come, Thou Fount of Every Blessing"
Robert Robinson (1735-1790)

Lord, we are sometimes too sure of our own wisdom and run ahead of you. We confuse our self-assurance with your wisdom. And we are especially prone to forget that our Saviour was poor and lowly, meek and gentle. Teach us to see you more clearly, love you more dearly, and follow you more nearly day by day. Amen.

14. KNOWING
WITHOUT GOING

News of the presence of question-asking foreigners had reached the Jerusalem palace. There was word on the street about a new star in the sky. And what was this talk about a new king of the Jews? Any one of these things would have troubled Herod; all three together precipitated a city-wide crisis.

You probably already know about King Herod. In some ways it is surprising that the Apostles' Creed, which many Christians recite every Sunday, mentions Pontius Pilate (Christ "suffered under Pontius Pilate") but makes no mention of the Herod family, under whom Jesus also suffered.

There is a reason why this Herod (several of them appear in the New Testament) is known as "the Great." His reign lasted some 37 years and was not without success; his special interest was in building projects, and these included the rebuilding of the Jerusalem Temple.

Herod was of Idumean (Edomite) descent, so he was not a "pure" Jew—in any sense. And it showed.

The infamous vicious streak of the English king Henry VIII pales by comparison with the ruthless brutalities of Herod. He executed one of his ten wives, three of his own sons, and hundreds of their supporters. Matthew's record of his violent response to news of a new king is wholly in character. Maintaining his throne was his priority—indeed his neurosis. No rivals were brooked.

All men are mortal; Herod was a man, and Herod was mortal. Already ill, he would be dead within a year or so. But he had no intention of letting the Herodian dynasty be replaced by any new king without a fight. His first move was to demand that the wise men be brought to a secret meeting.

We know from other sources that Herod often made use of people with exceptional ability. He could not have accomplished all he did in urban regeneration or in his massive building programmes otherwise. Even evil men know when they need advice. And in matters of religion and faith Herod had access to Jerusalem's leading theologians. So he assembled "the chief priests and the scribes of the people" (Matthew 2:4). These probably included the two most famous rabbis of the time: Hillel, the president of the Sanhedrin, and Shammai, its vice president. He "inquired of them" where the King of the Jews, the Messiah, was to be born (v 4).

These men probably knew much, if not all, of the Old Testament by heart. Perhaps they were able to give Herod the immediate answer: "In Bethlehem" (v 5). They could even give him chapter and verse: Micah, chapter 5, verse 2.

It is impressive that these men knew their Bibles so well.

But something else here leaves a deeper and sadder impression. Herod and his counsellors possessed what the wise men lacked—the Scriptures that spoke about Christ. But they lacked what the wise men had—the desire to find him.

The wise men were saying, *We believe the King of the Jews has been born; we don't know where, but wherever he is we want to go to reverence him.*

The religious leaders were saying, *We know where Messiah will be born, but we have no intention of going there.*

Any religious leader worth his salt should have said, *Bethlehem is only a few miles away; we'll take you. Let's go together!* But the prophecy of Micah made no more impact on them than if they had solved the morning-newspaper crossword puzzle or the daily sudoku. They answered Herod's question, packed up the scroll of Micah in its sacred container, and went home.

It is possible to know the Bible well and yet to be tone deaf to its message.

Perhaps, like me, you have experienced that tone deafness. I started reading the Bible when I was nine and continued to do so for the next five years, day in, day out. Of course, there are things in the Bible that a young boy will find difficult to understand. But I was learning what it was all about. Or so I thought, until one day I read these words of Jesus: "You search the Scriptures because you think that in them you have eternal life; and it is they that bear witness about me, yet you refuse to come to me that you may have life" (John 5:39-40). I saw it immediately: "This is me; this is where I am; he is talking to me; this is what I have done." It was as though the Lord Jesus himself walked off the page and addressed me personally and directly.

Knowing what is in the Bible, even not doubting its teaching, is not the same as finding and trusting Christ. The religious leaders' eyes could read the truth the Bible taught them, but their hearts were hardened. They saw no need to find Christ for themselves.

Don't let that be true of you. In this Christmas season—as we sing the same carols and listen to the same Bible passages, and hear sermons on the same familiar themes, and follow the same traditions as we have for many years—we are perhaps in more danger than at any other time of year of saying the right things with our lips without really engaging our hearts.

Meanwhile Herod's reaction was different again. He was incensed: *When I find out where Messiah has been born, I am going there—to destroy him.*

Three responses to the good news about Jesus Christ: we see them still today when people encounter him in his word or in the lives of Christians they know. A hunger to hear more; an indifference that passes itself off as sophistication; a hostility that manifests itself often in an antagonism to Christ, his people, the lifestyle he taught, and the exclusive claims he made about himself. True, this rejection is usually done in more subtle ways today than it was by King Herod or his theologians, but it is still done.

And, given the fact that books like this one sometimes end up in the hands of people who would not normally want to read them, perhaps this describes your response too.

There are only three responses you can make to Jesus Christ:

1. Learn about him and seek him—as the wise men.

2. Know about him but be indifferent to him—like the Jewish scholars.

3. Realise that he is the promised Saviour and King—but seek to destroy him as Herod did.

Which is yours?

⌒

In the streets I wandered slowly,
Looking for some trusty guide;
All was dark and melancholy,
None I met with, far and wide.
On a sudden I perceived
O'er my head a star to shine;
Lo, because I had believed,
And had sought him, Christ was mine!

Only seek and you will find him;
Never cease to seek the Lord;
And should he delay, remind him
Boldly of his plighted word.
Follow him, and he will lead you;

Trust him in the darkest night;
Jacob's star will still precede you,
Jacob's star will give you light.

"*Christ, Whose First Appearance Lighted –*
The Appearance of Christ"
C.J. Philipp Spitta (1801-1859)
Translated by Richard Massie (1800-1887)

Lord, today we may meet someone who is seeking you; help us to point them to you. Today we may meet someone who is indifferent to you; please let our lives speak of the wonder of knowing you. And if we should experience hostility to you, help us to imitate you so that someone may see you in our lives. Amen.

15. CAN YOU TRUST
A HEROD?

I was sitting in my college study-bedroom, reading John's Gospel, when some words arrested me. At first, they shocked me a little: "Jesus on his part did not entrust himself to them, because he knew all people ... he himself knew what was in man" (John 2:24).

A *non-trusting* Jesus? So it seems. Jesus welcomed all who came to him and received everyone who sought him. But he was not naïve. He saw beyond appearances and penetrated behind the masks people wear.

Growing Christians develop that kind of spiritual discernment. But it is understandable that the wise men lacked it. They were pagans. And now they had received a personal summons to meet no less a person than Herod the Great (Matthew 2:7). Surely, he would know the answers to their questions. So perhaps their journey was going to have a happy ending after all.

Had these ancient scholars already seen the temple that Herod had rebuilt? (They could hardly miss it in small-town Jerusalem.) If so, they would have been impressed. There was a rabbinical saying at the time: "The person who has not seen the temple of Herod has never seen a beautiful building." The builder of such an edifice surely had to be deeply religious, knowledgeable, and trustworthy.

If that was what the wise men thought, they could not have been more mistaken.

We know how the story ends; but these men didn't. We can see through Herod; but they couldn't. Perhaps they missed the tell-tale signs of his arrogance and ruthlessness. After all, he seemed interested; and he had gone to the trouble of researching the answer to their question *even before they met him.* Surely this was a man who would help?

You can imagine the conversation behind verses 7-8:

Herod: Approach and speak. I believe you are searching for someone.

Magi: Your Majesty—it is our honour to be received by you. We are scholars from the east. Some time ago we observed a new star. And then in our libraries we found records of ancient prophecies concerning a star symbolizing a new king arising among the Jewish people. Those records suggested he would be so great that his kingdom would extend to the ends of the earth and be greater than all other kingdoms. Thus, sire, we have come to honour the king of the Jews!

Herod: I too have a great interest in this king! When I heard of your presence in our city, I consulted my own wise men and scholars. They tell me that the

> *scroll of our prophet Micah states that his birth-*
> *place is Bethlehem. So, please, go there; search for*
> *him. And as soon as you find him, come back and*
> *tell me exactly where he is—so that I myself may*
> *go and worship him.*
>
> Magi: *Your Majesty has displayed an abundance of*
> *kindness to his humble servants. This we will*
> *surely do.*

They left for Bethlehem, apparently believing every word. They lacked the discernment to see through the king.

We can sympathise with these travellers; we would surely have done the same. All they had was a few dots. Even if they had joined them up, they would have seen only a fragment of the whole picture. They did not know that undergirding Micah's prophecy was a more ancient one, as old as the Garden of Eden. It too told of a conquering king whom God would send. But this king would have his heel bruised in the process of gaining his victory (Genesis 3:15). Had they known that the new king would be born into a vicious spiritual war, they might have been more watchful and on their guard.

What they did not know, Matthew knew. Later he would record Jesus' words to his disciple Peter: "I will build my church, and the gates of hell shall not prevail against it" (Matthew 16:18). Even so, hell would try.

And we also know this. We have the entire Bible. From beginning to end it tells a story of deceit and conflict in which every advance in God's purposes encounters opposition. Now the visitors from the east had unwittingly stumbled into a spiritual war zone, and they were in danger. It never crossed their mind that the new king would have enemies, and that one of them would be the old king. We can be grateful to God that he protected them.

This is not the last time in Matthew's story that we need to look beneath the surface to understand what is really happening. Immediately after our Lord's words about building his church in such a way that it would withstand hell's gates, he began to speak about the cross, saying that he would be killed (Matthew 16:21). Peter took Jesus aside and rebuked him for saying that he would suffer and die: "This shall never happen to you" (v 22). Jesus' response came with a sting: "Get behind me, Satan! You are a hindrance to me" (v 23). Peter should have known that, from as far back as Genesis 3:15, there was a spiritual war going on and that Jesus was the target, and that deception was one of the enemy's major weapons. But he had been blindsided. He had his mind set not "on the things of God, but on the things of man" (Matthew 16:23).

In a season awash with sentimentality, it is easy to be fooled that all around us is sweetness and light, and to expect nothing less than that for ourselves. Yet, as the great Dutch theologian Abraham Kuyper (one-time prime minister of the Netherlands) wisely wrote:

> *If once the curtain were pulled back, and the spiritual world behind it came to view, it would expose to our spiritual vision a struggle so intense, so convulsive, sweeping everything within its*

> *range, that the fiercest battle ever fought on earth*
> *would seem, by comparison, a mere game.*[6]

We simply must learn the lesson: the King has enemies, and therefore so do we. One of their well-tested weapons is deceiving Christians. We need to be on our guard.

> *And though this world with devils filled*
> *Should threaten to undo us,*
> *We will not fear, for God hath willed*
> *His truth to triumph through us.*
> *The prince of darkness grim,*
> *We tremble not for him;*
> *His rage we can endure,*
> *For lo! His doom is sure;*
> *One little word shall fell him.*

> *"A Mighty Fortress Is Our God"*
> *Martin Luther (1483-1546), translated by*
> *Frederick H. Hedge (1795-1881)*

Lord, you have taught us in your word that we are in a spiritual war, and that we must be on our guard lest we be deceived. But we are so weak and sometimes easily taken in. Teach us your word and give us wisdom. And meanwhile protect us today and help us to be on our guard. Amen.

---

6 Cited by G.C. Berkouwer, *A Half Century of Theology*, translated and edited by Lewis B. Smedes (Eerdmans, 1977), p 196.

16. FOLLOWING
A STAR

What are we to make of this "star"? It is mentioned only in Matthew's Gospel; but it continues to fascinate people. Every so often, an article appears in a theological or scientific journal suggesting its possible nature.

Was it a supernatural phenomenon created by God exclusively for the occasion? Matthew passes no comment. Down through the years perhaps three views have attracted most attention.

The first view is that what would have looked like a star to the wise men may in fact have been a conjunction of the planets Jupiter and Saturn. In antiquity Jupiter was the "royal" planet and Saturn represented "the west."

Imagine it like the British quiz game *Catchphrase*, where pictures taken together help the contestants guess a well-known expression. Here Jupiter and Saturn converge. The message? A king (Jupiter) is coming in the west (Saturn). Such a conjunction took place in 7 BC, which approximates to the year of Jesus' birth (King

Herod died in 4 BC, by which time Joseph and Mary had already spent some time in Egypt).

A second view is that it was a comet. We know that Halley's Comet appears every 75 years or so. It would have appeared around 12 BC, too early for the birth of Jesus. But comets can appear and then disappear for thousands of years. Perhaps this was one?

A third alternative is that it was a nova or super nova produced by a stellar explosion. What has made this view attractive is that such a phenomenon took place over a two-month period around 5 BC. This theory may sound very modern, but it goes back at least to the great astronomer Johannes Kepler (1571-1630). He is said to have written these beautiful words about his science: "I was merely thinking God's thoughts after him. Since we astronomers are priests of the highest God in regard to the book of nature, it benefits us to be thoughtful, not of the glory of our minds, but rather, above all else, of the glory of God."

These are theories. What is certain is that God employed a phenomenon in nature (the star was not a figment of their imagination!) to prompt the wise men to look for Jesus. The Scriptures show no special interest in the star's *nature*, only in its *significance*: it was going to lead these men to Jesus.

From Jerusalem the travellers then set off in a southerly direction towards Bethlehem. As night fell, they saw a welcome sight: the star was still there! "Behold, the star that they had seen when it rose went before them until it came to rest over the place where the child was. When they saw the star, they rejoiced exceedingly with great joy" (Matthew 2:9-10; that's a lot of joy).

Our Christmas cards sometimes give the impression that the star was hovering directly above the house where Mary and Joseph were then resident. But Matthew's account does not suggest such GPS accuracy. Objects in outer space do not hang above individual houses! The statement that the star "came to rest over the place where the child was" is probably a general reference to the fact that, heading south from Jerusalem, they saw the star directly aligned with Bethlehem.

This raises an interesting question. As the magi travelled south, a star that aligned with Bethlehem might also have aligned with other places, such as Hebron. The star on its own could hardly give them the confidence they needed. After all, if they had asked in Bethlehem, "Where is he who has been born king of the Jews?" a Bethlehem wit might have teasingly said, *Now, let's see, the last king who was born here was... Ah, yes— King David! You must have been travelling a long time; he's been dead for centuries!*

The wise men needed more than the star. God had used an astronomical event coupled perhaps with ancient prophecies to awaken their interest. But they needed more. And this alerts us to another remarkable element in God's providence. Just as he had overseen the twists and turns in Jesus' genealogy, he had now superintended the wise men's wandering into danger in Herod's palace to give them the final clue they needed: the teaching of Scripture!

That is always the key we need; for, without its teaching, whether we read it for ourselves or it is passed on to us by someone else, we can have no knowledge of Christ or his work as Messiah and Saviour. Without its testimony to him, we can never find him.

The experience of the wise men finding Christ in Bethlehem is unique, as is the story of Saul of Tarsus encountering him on the Damascus Road. These stories may seem much more supernatural than ours. But the truth is that while they may be more *dramatic*, ours are no less *supernatural*, for the same Lord sovereignly designed the events that also led us to faith. It was he who placed us in a Christian family, or brought us into contact with a Christian, or stirred up in us an unaccountable desire to read the Bible. He created in us a sense that there was something wrong or missing. And so, by various means, he brought us to the Bible's message and to faith in Christ.

The important thing is not how *spectacular* God's work is but how *effective* it has been. All that matters is that we have come to Christ, and have found in him what we were looking for, even if we did not at first know what that really was. And that is a reason to be profoundly thankful.

It is an amazing thought that thousands of people may be reading this book during Advent, and even reading this very page today. Perhaps one of them is experiencing what these wise men experienced: a searching for something that seems to be missing, the feeling that something is not quite right, or a new and unfamiliar sense of their sinfulness. Perhaps, already, they have started on a spiritual journey that has taken some twists and turns. But now it is becoming clear that what they need more than anything else is the Saviour, the King, Jesus.

Perhaps you are that person. Have you found him yet?

Brightest and best of the sons of the morning,
Dawn on our darkness, and lend us thine aid;
Star of the east, the horizon adorning,
Guide where our infant Redeemer is laid.

Say, shall we yield him in costly devotion
Odours of Edom and off'rings divine,
Gems of the mountain and pearls of the ocean,
Myrrh from the forest, or gold from the mine?

Vainly we offer each ample oblation,
Vainly with gifts would his favour secure;
Richer by far is the heart's adoration,
Dearer to God are the prayers of the poor.

"Brightest and Best"
Reginald Heber (1783-1826)

Lord, you know all of us who are reading these pages today. Please awaken in someone a new sense of need that will set them on a search to find you. And send help to them, whether through a Christian they meet or a desire to read the Bible you have inspired. Please bring someone to King Jesus today. Amen.

17. FINDING CHRIST

Matthew began his Gospel by inviting us to see the birth of Jesus through Joseph's eyes. But then his camera angle moved to an undisclosed location in the ancient Near East, and he invited us to look through the eyes of some ancient scholars.

What did they see? First, they saw a star and followed its path westwards; then they saw Herod the Great; then they saw the Scriptures, the prophecy of Micah; then they saw the star once again and followed it.

And here, in Matthew 2:11, they arrive in Bethlehem and at a specific house. What do they see now? "They saw the child with Mary his mother" (v 11).

This scene—a contender for the number one scene printed on Christmas cards—has often been portrayed by great artists and sculptors whose works have almost invariably been called "Madonna and Child" or "Virgin and Child." But that isn't the way Matthew puts it, is it? He says that what you see through the wise men's eyes is "the child with Mary his mother."

Matthew seems to insist on this. His order is not ac-cidental because he repeats these words—the child and his mother—another four times in the passage (Mat-thew 2:13, 14, 20, 21), in the same order each time. If you see the scene properly, the child comes first in your vision. He is small and, humanly speaking, helpless; but he takes centre stage.

Matthew provides his own commentary on these events by pointing us to Old Testament prophecies. He himself quotes from Isaiah, Jeremiah, and Hosea, as well as recording the words that Herod's counsellors quoted from Micah. And here, I suspect, his repeated use of the phrase "the child" was meant to remind his first readers and hearers (and us) of words found in the context of Isaiah 9:1-7 (from which he later quotes in Matthew 4:15-16):

> *For to us a child is born,*
> *to us a son is given …*
> *and his name shall be called*
> *Wonderful Counsellor, Mighty God,*
> *Everlasting Father, Prince of Peace.*
> *Of the increase of his government and of peace*
> *there will be no end,*
> *on the throne of David and over his kingdom,*
> *to establish it and to uphold it*
> *with justice and righteousness*
> *from this time forth and forevermore.*
> *The zeal of the* LORD *of hosts will do this.*
> *(Isaiah 9:6-7)*

This is *the child* the magi saw.

The eastern visitors now knew Micah 5:2. We have seen that they may also have been familiar with the contents of Numbers 24:17 and Daniel 7:13-28. The biblical picture was being built up for them. Did they perhaps ask Mary and Joseph if there were any more prophecies about the coming king? Certainly Matthew knew this prophecy in Isaiah; and Joseph and Mary would also have been familiar with it.

Isaiah had written that this "child" would bring about a great deliverance "as on the day of Midian" (Isaiah 9:4). He was referring to the "Battle of Midian," when, guided by God, Gideon had reduced his army in stages from 32,000 down to 300 men carrying 300 trumpets and 300 jars with torches inside them. They surrounded the Midianite camp by night, and then, on the signal, they smashed the jars—letting the light shine out—blew the trumpets, and shouted in triumph; the Midian army fled in disarray (Judges 7:1-25). Truly "the weakness of God is stronger than men" (1 Corinthians 1:25).

Perhaps Paul was thinking about this incident when he wrote about the light of the gospel shining in the darkness in the face of Jesus Christ, and he added, "We have this treasure in jars of clay to show that the surpassing power belongs to God and not to us" (2 Corinthians 4:7). For this child—"little, weak and helpless," as one carol puts it[7]—was nevertheless "Christ the power of God and the wisdom of God" (1 Corinthians 1:24). Truly, "the foolishness of God is wiser than men" (v 25).

---

7 "Once in Royal David's City" by Cecil Frances Alexander (1812-1895).

Isaiah saw that this child would be everything we lack. For our confusion, he is the "Wonderful Counsellor"; for our weakness, he is the "Mighty God"; for spiritual orphans and prodigal sons, he is the "Everlasting Father"; in our distress, he comes to us as the "Prince of Peace."

The travellers from the east were seeing more than they could take in when "going into the house they saw the child with Mary his mother." And Matthew, a Jew, is allowing us to see him through Gentile eyes. For Jesus is both the fulfilment of Jewish prophecy and the answer to Gentiles' longing.

The wise men could not have understood all this. But even what they did understand about the child led them to worship: "They fell down and worshipped him. Then, opening their treasures, they offered him gifts, gold and frankincense and myrrh" (Matthew 2:11).

There has been even more speculation about the wise men's gifts than about their names. One thing is certain: these were expensive presents, fit for a king. And although the child was found in modest—even impoverished—circumstances, they did not hesitate to open their treasures and offer them to him.

Look through the eyes of these scholars once more. Notice to whom they give their gifts: not to Joseph and Mary but to Jesus. Ordinarily you "offer" a spoonful of puréed food to a child. But these wise men had come not to feed him but to worship him. Their gifts were expressions of Jesus' royalty and perhaps their loyalty too. And they brought more than the gifts in their hands;

they offered themselves too: "They fell down and worshipped him."

The message seems obvious, doesn't it? When we see Christ, and when we recognise him as King, we too will fall down and worship him, and offer to him the richest treasures of our life—we lay at his feet the brightest and best of the things we hold dear.

Have you ever done that?

What would it look like to do that today?

Then did they know assuredly
Within that house, the King did lie;
One entered in then for to see,
And found the babe in poverty.

Then enter'd in those wise men three,
Full reverently upon their knee,
And offered there, in his presence,
Their gold, and myrrh, and frankincense.

Then let us all with one accord
Sing praises to our heavenly Lord,
That hath made heaven and earth of nought,
And with his blood mankind hath bought.

"The First Nowell," Traditional

Lord Jesus Christ, born a baby and yet a king, born in poverty and yet the one in whom are found all the treasures of wisdom and knowledge, receive both our lives and our gifts. And as you led men of old to worship you, lead us also by your Holy Spirit to bow before your throne and to offer to you the adoration of our hearts and lives. Amen.

18. A DIVINE
WARNING

Matthew doesn't tell us how long the wise men stayed on in Bethlehem. Don't you think they must have told Joseph and Mary the story of their journey, and wanted to hear their story too—and perhaps the story of the whole Bible?

They certainly stayed overnight, long enough for one of them (or was it Joseph?) to have a dream, warning them: *Don't go back to Herod* (Matthew 2:12). Perhaps that simply confirmed what they were beginning to suspect: he was not to be trusted. They bade farewell to Mary and Joseph and began the long journey home.

Matthew tells us no more. Nobody knows any more.

But what do we know? The Christmas-card scene of three men on camels reminds me of a poem I had to memorise in primary school about a pedlar: "Where he comes from nobody knows, or where he goes to, but on he goes" (*The Pedlar's Caravan* by W.B. Rands). But look at Matthew 2:1-12 in slow motion and it is surprising how much we do know about these scholars— enough to make for an interesting Christmas quiz:

How many facts do you know about the Magi? One point will be given for each correct answer. (Go on—give it a go before reading on!)

1. We know that they observed a new astronomical phenomenon.

2. We know that they interpreted this as a sign that a new king of the Jews had been born.

3. We know that this affected them in a way that was, apparently, not true of their colleagues and neighbours.

4. We know that they decided to set out on a long journey that took them eventually to Jerusalem and Bethlehem.

5. We know that, in preparation, they either purchased or gathered together several expensive gifts to present to the new king.

6. We know that en route they made enquiries about the new king.

7. We know that news about them reached the ears of King Herod.

8. We know that their questions disturbed Herod.

9. We know that Herod's reputation for cruelty was such that this had a ripple effect on the citizens of Jerusalem.

10. We know that in preparation for interviewing them, Herod summoned the religious leaders to ask about the birth of the Messiah.

11. We know that Herod called them to a secret meeting.

12. We know that Herod sent them to Bethlehem.

13. We know that they were thrilled when they discovered that the star could still be seen.

14. We know that they realised that it was aligned with Bethlehem.

15. We know that there, in Bethlehem, they found the King who was the reason for their journey.

16. We know that they presented to the child the gifts they had brought for him.

17. We know they bowed down and worshipped him.

18. We know they stayed overnight and probably had extended conversations with Mary and Joseph.

19. We know they were warned through a dream not to report back to Herod.

20. We know that they went home by a route avoiding Jerusalem.

What can we learn from all this? One lesson is obvious: from Matthew's perspective, the Lord's hand had clearly been on these men from the very beginning of the story. God worked out his purposes through an unusual providence in the magi's ordinary working lives combined with an inner personal compulsion to respond to it. And over a period of time he brought them to Christ.

There was something unique about the wise men's experience. But we can also trace a pattern. An *awakening* takes place, and then a *drawing*, and then a *discovering*, and then a *worshipping*.

At the end of a series of lunchtime services in the city-centre church in which I served, a young woman handed me a thick envelope. Many preachers are so conscious of their weaknesses that they develop a dread of a thick envelope being handed to them—chances are that it is a letter of complaint! But this one told the story of a young research scientist. Sitting in her university lab nearby, she became conscious that every Wednesday at 1.00 p.m. our church bell began to toll. It was not simply the clock chiming 1.00 p.m., because the bell kept ringing after that time. It felt like a summons—and when she realised that, she consciously resisted it week after week.

Then, one day, her letter said, she found herself sitting in the service which the bell announced. Like someone who realises they have driven the last ten miles on the road without being conscious of it, she couldn't really remember getting up from her bench, leaving the lab, and walking the half mile down the street. But she did. And that day she came to faith in Christ. Now, weeks later, she wanted to share her story.

We might call this "the wise-men pattern" (or, in the researcher's case, "the wise-woman pattern"). Something stirs us spiritually, although we hardly realise it. Whatever grips us doesn't necessarily affect others in the same way. Perhaps we resist, or take a wrong turning, thinking we can work things out on our own. But then, somehow, through a Christian we know or a compulsion to read the Bible for ourselves, we are led to Christ.

Different people, different cultures, different centuries, different personal narratives—and yet the same pattern of being brought to faith.

No wonder we love the story of the wise men from the east! The Lord had his hand on them, just as he has had his hand on us. And so we can look in hope for the ways in which he has his hand on the lives of non-believers whom we know and love.

There's another lesson here. But it must wait for the final chapter of the story of the magi.

⌐⎯⎯⎯⌐

As with gladness men of old
Did the guiding star behold,
As with joy they hailed its light,
Leading onward, beaming bright,
So, most gracious Lord, may we
Evermore be led to thee.

Holy Jesus, every day
Keep us in the narrow way;
And when earthly things are past,

Bring our ransomed souls at last
Where they need no star to guide,
Where no clouds thy glory hide.

"As with Gladness Men of Old"
William Chatterton Dix (1837-1898)

Our Father, we can never thank you enough for the way in which you awakened us from spiritual slumber. You called some of us with a gentle whisper, and on others you threw cold water! But you knew exactly what was needed to bring us to trust in the Lord Jesus. Thank you! Thank you! Amen.

PART 4

THE JOURNEYS

MATTHEW 2:13-23

¹³ Now when they had departed, behold, an angel of the Lord appeared to Joseph in a dream and said, "Rise, take the child and his mother, and flee to Egypt, and remain there until I tell you, for Herod is about to search for the child, to destroy him." ¹⁴ And he rose and took the child and his mother by night and departed to Egypt ¹⁵ and remained there until the death of Herod. This was to fulfil what the Lord had spoken by the prophet, "Out of Egypt I called my son."

¹⁶ Then Herod, when he saw that he had been tricked by the wise men, became furious, and he sent and killed all the male children in Bethlehem and in all that region who were two years old or under, according to the time that he had ascertained from the wise men. ¹⁷ Then was fulfilled what was spoken by the prophet Jeremiah:

¹⁸ "A voice was heard in Ramah,
weeping and loud lamentation,
Rachel weeping for her children;
she refused to be comforted, because they
are no more."

¹⁹ But when Herod died, behold, an angel of the Lord appeared in a dream to Joseph in Egypt, ²⁰ saying, "Rise, take the child and his mother and go to the land of Israel, for those who sought the child's life are dead." ²¹ And he rose and took the child and his mother and went to the land of Israel. ²² But when he heard that Archelaus was reigning over Judea in place of his father Herod, he was afraid to go there, and being warned in a dream he withdrew to the district of Galilee. ²³ And he went and lived in a city called Nazareth, so that what was spoken by the prophets might be fulfilled, that he would be called a Nazarene.

19. LONG JOURNEYS

For many of us, Christmas is a time for making long journeys. These days in December are usually some of the busiest on the roads as families criss-cross their way around the country. When you are travelling, do you sometimes find yourself watching other people's faces and guessing what their expressions tell you about them? Is he stressed? Is she excited? He looks bored!

These verses in Matthew are likewise full of criss-crossing journeys, which will be the focus of our studies over the next days. First, the wise men. As the magi's camels slowly made their way out of Bethlehem at the beginning of their long journey home, what might the expressions of their riders have given away?

Satisfaction, perhaps? They had set out guided by a heavenly body; they had reached their intended destination guided by a Jewish prophecy; they had found the king for whom they were looking. The mission, from that point of view, had been successful.

Or perhaps they were perplexed. Their quest had precipitated a conflict situation that they could not have anticipated. Even more unexpected—the newborn king was not a palace resident. His crib had been a manger. The "princess" who gave birth to him was in fact the teenage wife of a carpenter husband. Yet, unlike the occupant of the Jerusalem palace, this little family could trace their lineage all the way back to Israel's King David. It seemed that the wise men had discovered the rightful heir to David's throne. Yet he had been born into obscurity. And now they were leaving him knowing that his life and his parents' lives, and perhaps even their own lives, were under threat.

They had found what they sought. They left with thoughts they would ponder for the rest of their lives. They could have written, well in advance of William Shakespeare, "There's a divinity that shapes our ends, rough hew them how we will" (*Hamlet*, Act V, Scene 2).

These scholars must have asked themselves what kind of king this child would be. What destiny lay ahead of him? Imagine the conversations they must have had on the way home as they tried to piece together what they had learned about him!

It may be that the wise men had even more than that to ponder. Matthew and Luke tell the nativity story from different perspectives, reflecting the memories of different people. Neither of them makes any attempt to provide all the details. But the chronology seems to have been like this:

1. Joseph and Mary journey to Bethlehem.

2. Jesus is born.

3. Shepherds from the fields around Bethlehem come to see him.

4. A week later Jesus is circumcised and officially named.

5. A few weeks later a visit to Jerusalem takes place for Mary's purification (Luke 2:22).

6. The little family returns to Bethlehem and now finds a house in which they can stay.

7. The wise men arrive.

According to this chronology, Joseph and Mary would have been in Jerusalem before the visit of the wise men. There they had met the two elderly saints, Simeon and Anna.

By another "secret instinct of the Spirit," Simeon had recognised the baby Jesus as the Messiah and had spoken of his future glory. But he had also given a hint of the suffering that lay ahead for both Jesus and his mother: "Behold, this child is appointed for the fall and rising of many in Israel, and for a sign that is opposed (and a sword will pierce through your own soul also)" (Luke 2:34-35). What consolation it must have been to Mary (and perhaps to Joseph too) that Anna, long widowed and therefore familiar with pain and grief, was there to reassure them (v 36-38).

Had Mary and Joseph shared all this with the wise men? And did they therefore learn not only of the future glory of the infant king they had worshipped but also of his future suffering? Did Mary and Joseph tell them about Isaiah's prophecy of the Servant who would be exalted over the nations, but only after his rejection and death (Isaiah 52:13 – 53:12)?

If so, the returning scholars had much to ponder, and much still to discuss and try to understand en route home. They now had in their possession the two central threads in the tapestry of the gospel. But were they able to weave them together to see that what lay ahead was the child's death and resurrection?

How much they understood would depend on how much Joseph and Mary understood and were able to explain. (We know that Mary pondered this a great deal, Luke 2:19.) But doesn't this conjure up a wonderful scene—this peasant couple and these eastern intellectuals sitting at each other's feet, comparing notes, and trying to understand the gospel?

Within a day or two all of them were gone—the cosy scene shattered by dreams warning of danger. The men headed back east, while Joseph and his little family headed south, no doubt all of them travelling along roads that would help them to avoid detection by Herod. The sword was already piercing Mary's soul; the shadow of the cross was already falling on the child.

The wise men and the parents shared one thing in common: knowing Jesus means taking up the cross and following him. Yes, there had been a price to pay for the wise men's long journey westwards; but there was a different kind of cost now. And for Mary and Joseph, life could never be the same again. They would all discover that the shadow of the cross that fell on the child would also touch them. The same is true for his followers today. Have you felt that shadow? Are you willing to?

Each of the people gathered in that house in Bethlehem gave Jesus all they had. His parents gave their lives to him; the magi gave their precious gifts. But surely they all left Bethlehem with a sense that "he is no fool, who parts with that which he cannot keep, when he is sure to be recompensed with that which he cannot lose."[8]

What child is this, who, laid to rest,
On Mary's lap is sleeping?
Whom angels greet with anthems sweet,
While shepherds watch are keeping?
This, this, is Christ the King,
Whom shepherds guard and angels sing:
Haste, haste, to bring him laud,
The babe, the son of Mary

So bring him incense, gold, and myrrh;
Come peasant, king, to own him;
The King of kings salvation brings,
Let loving hearts enthrone him.
Raise, raise the song on high,

---

8 The words are those of Philip Henry, recorded by his son, the famous Bible commentator Matthew Henry. See Matthew Henry, *The Life of the Rev. Philip Henry* (John P. Haven, AM Tract House, 1830), p 75.

The virgin sings her lullaby:
Joy, joy for Christ is born,
The babe, the son of Mary.

"What Child Is This?"
Traditional

Lord Jesus, you gave yourself without reservation for us; throughout the years you have enabled your disciples to bear the cross. Support and strengthen us that we may serve you well, whatever the cost. Take our lives, and our gifts, because we lay them at your feet for your glory. Amen.

20. OUT OF EGYPT

The warning that accelerated the wise men's homeward journey was soon followed by another dream and another flight. An angel appeared in Joseph's dream, warning him that Herod's search-and-destroy team was about to arrive in Bethlehem: "Rise, take the child and his mother, and flee to Egypt, and remain there until I tell you, for Herod is about to search for the child, to destroy him" (Matthew 2:13). They needed to leave *immediately*. *Head south to Egypt, and don't leave there until I tell you!* No territory governed by Herod was safe for them. And so they became refugees in Egypt.

Most of us think of Egypt as far away. But it's only far away from where we are! If you look at a map, you'll see that it would have taken only a few days more for Joseph and Mary to get to the Egyptian border than to go north to Nazareth. Herod wouldn't have expected them to leave the country. And in Egypt they would have been outside his territories altogether. Still, even getting to the border was a week's journey—and a week must seem a long time when there is a price on your head.

Judging by the media reports, when religious leaders preach on this passage at Christmas time, the sermon usually has something to do with the number of refugees in the world, and shame on us (or our governments) if we ignore them. Granted, this is a tragic situation—but it isn't Matthew's point. He is not telling the story to evoke pity for this little family or to shame governments into doing more for today's refugees. His real point is to tell us something about Jesus.

Sometimes it's amazing how easily we miss the point.

Years ago, during a Sunday-evening service, about fifteen minutes after it had started, an entire troop of visitors entered the gallery and tried to find seats. They were very obviously from somewhere in the Middle East. My immediate thought was that the sermon title—on the Trinity—had attracted a group of Muslims. But chatting to them afterwards, I discovered they were Coptic Christians from Egypt: teachers who had been sponsored to attend a several-weeks-long in-service course at one of the city's universities. To our delight, they continued to come until their course ended. The presence of so many Egyptian Copts was an unusual and enriching experience for a Presbyterian church!

We had many conversations with our delightful guests. But two stick out, partly because, I think, they took place on the same evening.

In the first conversation, one of the Egyptian friends spoke to me with enthusiasm about the Lord Jesus. In the second conversation, shortly afterwards, another teacher, speaking with no less enthusiasm, asked me if I knew that the holy family had visited Egypt. (I did—Matthew chapter 2!) "Well then," my new friend told me, "You must visit Egypt to see some of the food of the holy family that has been miraculously preserved!"

In a short space of time, these two conversations illustrated to me the difference between a Christ-full Christianity and a sentimental one. One man saw the Bread of life in Egypt; the other saw only bread.

Here, Matthew wants us to see Jesus as he is. The point in this story of Egyptian exile is about Jesus' identity; for, later, once Herod was dead, Jesus would be brought out of Egypt, and thus "fulfil what the Lord had spoken by the prophet, 'Out of Egypt I called my son'" (Matthew 2:15). The words are a quotation from Hosea 11:1, which reflects on the rescue of God's people—his "son" Israel—from slavery in Egypt.

As we listen to the different movements in what we might call "Matthew's Symphony," there is a melody playing in the background drawn, as it were, from "Moses' Symphony." There are echoes of the story told in Genesis and Exodus. A family goes down into Egypt; a child is rescued from a wicked ruler; he grows up and leads his people out of their bondage; they pass through the waters of the sea; they are tested in the wilderness; eventually they reach the borders of the promised land.

These events are like a shadow cast backwards into history from the life of our Lord. He is the reality. He is the true Son of God who was called out of Egypt; he would go through the waters in his baptism in the River Jordan (Matthew 3:1-17); he would be tested in the wilderness (4:1-11).

Matthew is telling us that in Jesus a greater exodus has begun. 30 years later, on the Mount of Transfiguration, Jesus would discuss with Moses and Elijah the "departure" (literally the "exodus," Luke 9:31) that he was about to accomplish in Jerusalem. This true and final exodus would not be a physical deliverance from an earthly pharaoh. Nor would it be freedom from merely physical servitude. It would be deliverance from Satan, and from the guilt, and power, and shame of sin.

Jesus being taken into Egypt was not simply for his own safety. It was to fulfil a prophecy—to fill out and fill up a pattern that God had written into his own people's history to point them forward to the full and final exodus that would bring us eternal salvation. And brought it he has. Now there is no earthly danger, worldly power, or spiritual snare that his people need to fear.

Everywhere we look in this story, we discover that it is all about salvation. That is its central message. That is the Christmas message. And it is our greatest need. If only we would see it!

Forth today the Conqueror goeth,
Who the foe, sin and woe,
Death and hell o'erthroweth,
God is man, man to deliver;

His dear Son now is one
With our blood for ever.

Hark! A voice from yonder manger,
Soft and sweet, doth entreat:
"Flee from woe and danger.
Brethren, from all ills that grieve you,
You are freed; all you need
I will surely give you."

"All My Heart This Night Rejoices"
Paul Gerhardt (1607-76), translated by
Catherine Winkworth (1829-1878)
Altered.

Heavenly Father, what trials and opposition our Lord Jesus experienced. How much you must love us, that you sent your only Son into exile for us. Thank you that he came so willingly, and that he has brought us out of our sinful exile and into the light and life of his grace. Amen.

21. THE CHILD
POGROM

As the wise men were heading east, and Joseph and his little family were now on their way south, another group could be seen getting ready to make a sinister journey from further north. Soldiers from Herod's palace were being mustered to travel quickly down the Jerusalem-Bethlehem road. They constituted an execution squad:

> *Then Herod, when he saw that he had been*
> *tricked by the wise men, became furious, and*
> *he sent and killed all the male children in*
> *Bethlehem and in all that region who were two*
> *years old and under, according to the time that*
> *he had ascertained from the wise men.*
>
> *(Matthew 2:16)*

Matthew 2:16-18 leaves a bad taste in the mouth. True, the extent of Herod's pogrom was certainly not as massive as the medieval carols suggest, for Bethlehem was only a small town with perhaps a thousand inhabitants. There would have been a relatively small number of boys aged two and under in the region. But each of them was a beloved son, perhaps a brother, or a grandson: a little person well-known as he played in the streets or was seen with his family. And every one of them was viciously deprived of life. The Lord Jesus never met another man from the town of Bethlehem who was his exact contemporary.

There is no record of this event outside of Matthew's Gospel. But there is no reason to doubt his words. This is what Herod's track record would lead you to expect. He had the blood of a multitude on his hands. To crown his cruelty, he arranged for a substantial number of men to be executed on the day he died. He planned to guarantee that there would be genuine mourning throughout the land. Thankfully, he was not alive to effect his orders. But no wonder Augustus Caesar is reputed to have said that it would be preferable to be Herod's pig than one of his sons.

Couldn't we somehow have lingered longer on the earlier parts of Matthew's story, so that in these final days before Christmas, we would be thinking about the magi? Then we could close the book and enjoy Christmas Day.

We probably could have. After all, the other Gospel writers omit these ghastly details. But if we skipped these verses, we would be missing something that *Matthew* wants to tell us.

Embedded in Matthew's Gospel from the very beginning is the message that Jesus the Saviour is for all the nations. Matthew begins with the Saviour's family tree punctuated by Gentile women, tells us about Gentile scholars from the east seeking him, and then records Jesus himself being carried to the land of Egypt. And the Gospel ends with him sending his apostles to make disciples of "all nations." His birth has worldwide significance. To use the language of Revelation, Jesus has come so that "Satan ... might not deceive the nations any longer" (Revelation 20:2-3).

It is against this background that Matthew records how Satan tempted Jesus (Matthew 4:1-11); how one of his own disciples sought to divert him (16:21-23); how religious leaders plotted against him (21:45; 26:3-5); how another of his disciples betrayed him (26:14-16); and eventually how his enemies, spiritually blinded, crucified the Lord of glory (26:47 – 27:50; see 1 Corinthians 2:8).

We have seen the explanation for this. At the centre of Matthew's Gospel stands Jesus' vision statement: "I will build my church" (Matthew 16:18). He does this on enemy-occupied territory in the face of "the gates of hell." Even so, he assures us, they "shall not prevail."

But it will not be for want of trying. Herod's murder of these little boys tells us how vicious Satan's opposition to Jesus is. This was the opening salvo of a war that would be waged against our Lord for the rest of his life. Herod himself was but a lieutenant in the history-long strategy of Satan to prevent Jesus accomplishing what he came into the world to do: namely, "save his people from their sins" (1:21).

What happened in Bethlehem therefore was yet another stage in the conflict that God had announced in Genesis 3:15. The seed of the serpent would oppose and eventually seek to crush the seed of the woman. The story that began in Genesis 3:15 was now running on through Matthew 2:1-17 and 16:18 to its climax. John saw this conflict in dramatic and symbolic form in the Book of Revelation:

> *And a great sign appeared in heaven: a woman*
> *clothed with the sun, with the moon under her*
> *feet, and on her head a crown of twelve stars. She*
> *was pregnant and was crying out in birth pains*
> *and the agony of giving birth. And another sign*
> *appeared in heaven: behold, a great red dragon,*
> *with seven heads and ten horns, and on his heads*
> *seven diadems. His tail swept down a third of*
> *the stars of heaven and cast them to the earth.*
> *And the dragon stood before the woman who*
> *was about to give birth, so that when she bore*
> *her child he might devour it. She gave birth to*
> *a male child, one who is to rule all the nations*
> *with a rod of iron, but her child was caught up*
> *to God and to his throne. (Revelation 12:1-5)*

The "great red dragon" was "that ancient serpent, who is called the devil and Satan, the deceiver of the whole world" (v 9). And now, in the real-time version of John's vision, the child had been born. The coming of the wise men was the first hint that the undeceiving of the nations had begun. And so the evil one let loose his dupe, King Herod, against the child.

We now live at a different point of John's vision: "The dragon became furious with the woman and went off to make war on the rest of her offspring, on those who keep the commandments of God and hold to the testimony of Jesus" (v 17). Perhaps, as you look at the world around you today, it feels as though the dragon must be winning—as Christians around the world suffer attack and harassment, as non-Christians hear the gospel yet remain blind to the message, and as Satan accuses and tempts you on the battle ground of your own heart. Yet however fierce the heat, hold on to our Saviour's promise: "I will the build my church, and the gates of hell shall not prevail against it" (Matthew 16:18).

As we close, we should take one final look at King Herod, since here in Matthew 2 is the last time we will meet him. He is faced with a choice. He has heard that the long-promised Messiah, King, and Saviour has come. He has only two alternatives:

1. He can yield to him, go with the wise men to find him, worship him, and open his treasures to him as his Saviour and King. *Or...*

2. He can resist him and do everything in his power to destroy him.

He now had no other choice. There was still hope for Herod until this point; but then all hope came to an end. "Unless you believe that I am he," Jesus would later say, "you will die in your sins" (John 8:24). Everything we know about the last days of Herod the Great suggests that he did die in his sins.

Please don't be like him: not while you are still reading this book. For no matter who you are or what you may have done, Jesus promises you, "Whoever comes to me I will never cast out" (6:37)—no matter how great your past resistance to him has been.

Hark the glad sound! The Saviour comes,
The Saviour promised long;
Let every heart prepare a throne,
And every voice a song.

He comes the prisoners to release,
In Satan's bondage held;
The gates of brass before him burst,
The iron fetters yield.

He comes the broken heart to bind,
The bleeding soul to cure,
And with the treasures of his grace
To enrich the humble poor.

Our glad hosannas, Prince of Peace,
Thy welcome shall proclaim;
And heaven's eternal arches ring
With thy belovèd name.

"Hark the Glad Sound!"
Philip Doddridge (1702-1751)

Lord, search our hearts, and cleanse them. Expose within us any lingering opposition to you so that we may confess it and drink deeply from the rivers of forgiveness that flow to us from your Son, Jesus. We ask it in his name. Amen.

22. ANOTHER PROPHECY FULFILLED

Christmas has a way of bringing our grief into focus. We know families for whom this year's festivities will be touched with sadness. Perhaps your family is one of them. Matthew's nativity account is a reminder to us that the first Christmas not only brought joy; it also involved lament. As the soldiers invaded Bethlehem to fulfil Herod's evil decree…

> *then was fulfilled what was spoken by the prophet Jeremiah:*
> *"A voice was heard in Ramah,*
> * weeping and loud lamentation,*
> *Rachel weeping for her children;*
> * she refused to be comforted, because they are*
> *no more." (Matthew 2:17-18)*

What did Matthew mean by saying that the words of Jeremiah 31:15 were fulfilled? Jeremiah was describing the tragic scene of the people of God being gathered together at Ramah to begin the long march that would take them into exile. The significance of Ramah was that it lay in the territory of Benjamin, where Rachel's tomb was (1 Samuel 10:2). We read in Genesis 35:16-18 of how she, Jacob, and their family had been travelling from Bethel on the road to Bethlehem when Rachel went into labour. She died shortly after childbirth, but not before naming her son "Ben-oni" ("son of my sorrow"). Jacob, courageously, renamed him "Ben-jamin", meaning "son of my right hand."

Rachel's sorrow—her "weeping" in Ramah—was because she knew she would never see her children again. Over 1,000 years later, in Jeremiah's time, it was as though it was happening all over again in the exile. It looked as if these children of the patriarchs would never be seen again in the land God had promised to give them.

Now, in Matthew 2, it was not a foreign conqueror who was seeking to destroy the hope of Israel but their own king. A pattern was being repeated, but this time the stakes were higher. Now the risk was not simply the destruction of the people's hope in the covenant promise but the destruction of the promised child, who was *himself* the covenant of God. As Matthew thought of the weeping mothers of these dear boys, no wonder he saw this child massacre in Bethlehem as the ultimate fulfilment of the ancient pattern.

But that's not the only thing we can take from Matthew's quotation of Jeremiah 31:15. When the New Testament writers quote the Old Testament, they usually seem to assume that their readers will be familiar with the original context of the quotation. If you know the "big passages" in the Old Testament, just saying "Jeremiah 31" rings a bell. Its later verses are alluded to, or directly quoted, more than ten times in the New Testament:

> *Behold, the days are coming, declares the Lord,*
> *when I will make a new covenant ... I will put*
> *my law within them, and I will write it on their*
> *hearts. And I will be their God and they shall*
> *be my people ... For I will forgive their iniquity,*
> *and I will remember their sin no more.*
>
> *(Jeremiah 31:31-34)*

For all the darkness of Jeremiah's earlier words and their application to the Bethlehem pogrom, is Matthew assuming that our minds and memories will run on to the new covenant promise? As in Jeremiah's day, so too in the days of the Bethlehem infanticide: there is hope. For the promised child, whom the serpent has sought to crush, has been protected. And one day he will crush the serpent. Yes, in the process his own heel will be crushed (Genesis 3:15), but the blood he sheds will be that of a new covenant. Yes, Rachel weeps, and Bethlehem despairs; but God will keep his covenant promise. For all his promises will find their ultimate "yes" in Jesus Christ (2 Corinthians 1:20).

In his imaginative epic poem "The Innkeeper," John Piper envisages the Lord Jesus returning to Bethlehem two weeks before his crucifixion. There he meets Jacob (the innkeeper) who had given shelter to Joseph and Mary when Jesus was born. His two little boys, Ben and Joseph, and his wife, Rachel, had been slaughtered by Herod's soldiers; Jacob himself had been wounded trying to protect them. He wonders why the Messiah had not come to save them:

> *"I lost*
> *My arm, my wife, my sons—the cost*
> *For housing the Messiah here.*
> *Why would he simply disappear*
> *And never come to help?"*
> *They sat*
> *In silence. Jacob wondered at*
> *The stranger's tears.*
> *"I am the boy*
> *That Herod wanted to destroy.*
> *You gave my parents room to give*
> *Me life, and then God let me live,*
> *And took your wife. Ask me not why*
> *The one should live, another die.*
> *God's ways are high, and you will know*
> *In time. But I have come to show*
> *You what the Lord prepared the night*
> *You made a place for heaven's light.*
> *In two weeks they will crucify*
> *My flesh. But mark this, Jacob, I*
> *Will rise in three days from the dead,*
> *And place my foot upon the head*
> *Of him who has the power of death,*
> *And I will raise with life and breath*
> *Your wife and Ben and Joseph too*

> *And give them, Jacob, back to you*
> *With everything the world can store,*
> *And you will reign for evermore.* "[9]

I wonder how many fathers in Bethlehem remembered the words of their town's most famous son—the great King David, who himself lost a child?

> *David said to his servants, "Is the child dead?"*
> *They said, "He is dead." ... [David said] "I shall*
> *go to him, but he will not return to me."*
> *(2 Samuel 12:19, 23)*

Years later, when David faced his own death, he repeated again his faith in God's word: "He has made with me an everlasting covenant, ordered in all things and secure" (2 Samuel 23:5). So, too, the mothers and fathers of Bethlehem could place their hope in God's promise.

In whatever way death casts its shadow on us this Christmas, we too can find comfort and assurance in God's unbreakable covenant with us. And as we remember the grieving parents of Bethlehem, we can pray ourselves for the little ones we know, in the words of this hymn by Thomas Haweis:

> *Our children, Lord, in faith and prayer,*
> *We now devote to thee;*
> *Let them thy covenant mercies share,*
> *And thy salvation see.*

---

9 John Piper, *The Innkeeper* (Crossway, 2011).

⸺

They scarcely waked before they slept,
They scarcely wept before they laughed;
They drank indeed death's bitter draught,
But all its bitterest dregs were kept
  And drained by Mothers while they wept.

From Heaven the speechless Infants speak:
Weep not (they say), our Mothers dear,
For swords nor sorrows come not here.
Now we are strong who were so weak,
  And all is ours we could not seek.

"They Scarcely Waked Before They Slept"
Christina G Rossetti (1830-1894)

⸺

Father, there is an agony in reading these words. They remind us of how cruel life can be, and with what unexplained tragedies so many have to live. Help us to understand how fierce is Satan's hatred of your goodness and love. And help us, we pray, to spread the comfort of the good news of your salvation in Jesus Christ. Amen.

23. SAFE TO GO HOME?

For all the joy of giving gifts to our children, the last couple of days before Christmas can be filled with more than their share of stress. In a way, that is a parable of life in general, isn't it? It is joy *and* stress. That is certainly true if you are a parent because your relationships with your children amount to far more than giving them toys on Christmas morning—the responsibility is enormous because they breathe in the atmosphere you breathe out every single day.

All parents shape their children in profound ways—for good or, as appears to have been the case in King Herod's family, for ill.

In the spring of the year 4 BC, the announcement came from the royal palace at Jericho: "King Herod is dead." He had been bitter and vicious to the end, but now the monster who had tried to destroy the Son of God was no more; and once again "an angel of the Lord appeared in a dream to Joseph" (Matthew 2:19) It was time to go home; their refugee existence was over.

But where was home?

After Herod's death the Emperor Augustus divided up his territories into three sections, each under the rule of one of his sons: Archelaus, Philip, and Antipas. Archelaus went to Rome, accompanied by Antipas, to dispute the terms of their father's will. (He had made six different ones!) At Passover, just before he left for Rome, he had some 3,000 people killed. As Joseph and Mary travelled north, they heard that Archelaus was now governing Judaea. So long as that was true, there would be no safe house for them there. So they by-passed Bethlehem and headed north to Galilee.

The Lord Jesus would never be free of the Herod family. Herod the Great stands at the beginning; Herod Antipas is there at the end (Luke 23:6-9). In that sense the Gospel narrative contains a tale of two families who, at times, cross paths: the Herod family on the one hand and Jesus and his spiritual family on the other.

We've already seen how Herod the father was once in the presence of a group of eastern scholars who, had he desired, could have brought him to Christ (Matthew 2:7). But he sought to destroy him.

30 years later, Herod the son was in the presence of John the Baptist (14:3-4)—a man who could have told him, "Behold, the Lamb of God, who takes away the sin of the world" (John 1:29). But he had him executed.

Not so long afterwards, having wanted to meet Jesus (Luke 9:9)—but, like his father before him, planning to kill him (13:31)—Antipas was finally in the presence of the Lamb of God himself, as Jesus stood trial before him (23:6-11). But nothing had changed—except, perhaps, that now Antipas was a man with a seared conscience. He felt nothing in the presence of the Son of God except a desire to see him perform some sign for his entertainment. And failing to receive one, "Herod with his soldiers treated him with contempt and mocked him. Then, arraying him in splendid clothing, he sent him back to Pilate" (23:11).

Herod Antipas treated the Lord Jesus as "a lamb that is led to the slaughter." But, adds Isaiah, "he opened not his mouth" (Isaiah 53:7). Despite all Herod's questions to him, Jesus "made no answer" (Luke 23:9). Now the time had come when Jesus had nothing more to say to him than, by implication, "I never knew you" (Matthew 7:23).

A few years later, the Roman Emperor Caligula banished Herod Antipas to what is now France—on the accusation of the emperor's friend, Herod's own nephew!

The Acts of the Apostles later introduces us to that nephew: Herod Agrippa I, grandson of Herod the Great. He persecuted the church (Acts 12:1); he had James, the brother of John, executed (v 2). He arrested Peter (v 3), who was delivered on the evening of his probable execution by a remarkable angelic visitation (v 6-17). In retaliation Herod executed the prison guards (v 19).

Soon afterwards, as he sat in royal council, people—no doubt cowed by his viciousness—acclaimed him: "The voice of a god, and not of a man!" But now the end came: "Immediately an angel of the Lord struck him down, because he did not give God the glory, and he was eaten by worms and breathed his last. But the word of God increased and multiplied" (v 23-24).

And finally in Acts we meet Herod's great-grandson, Herod Agrippa II, who taunted Paul with the words, "In a short time would you persuade me to be a Christian?" (26:28).

In telling the story of Herod's family and their persecution of Christ and his church, the New Testament indicates that the history-long conflict between the seed of the serpent and the seed of the woman was continuing—but also that the victory of the Seed of the woman was secure.

We use the expression "like father, like son." It can be true spiritually as well as physically. What the father breathes out the sons breathe in. It was so, alas, in the Herod family. Thankfully, in God's grace, there are exceptions.

People often say, "Christmas is for the children." In some ways that is a truism; but there is a sense in which it should be profoundly true; for, if we are parents, what will we give to our children this Christmas? What Herod the Great seems to have given his sons at the first Christmas was an example of hatred of the Lord Jesus. And, alas, his sons eagerly opened and used the present.

Instead, will we give our children an example of love for Jesus this Christmas? It is the best present they could receive. It is a wonderful thing at Christmas time to want to give your children a home where Jesus is welcomed and an example of a life devoted to him. What would it look like to intentionally go about that over the next few days?

I suppose there may well be descendants of Herod the Great somewhere in the world. But I suspect you do not know any of the family. By contrast, you probably know dozens if not hundreds, perhaps even thousands, of the millions of members of Jesus' spiritual family. What a privilege for our children to belong to it too!

Yes, in that sense, "Christmas is for the children." So, whether or not we are parents, today is a great day to be thankful for what one of my former colleagues often called "the worldwide, eternity-long family of God."

And perhaps if you are a Christian parent, before the rush of the next 24 hours, this would be a good time to recommit yourself to blessing your own children with what truly matters this Christmas.

Away in a manger, no crib for a bed,
The little Lord Jesus laid down his sweet head.
The stars in the bright sky
Looked down where he lay,
The little Lord Jesus asleep on the hay.

The cattle are lowing, the baby awakes,
But little Lord Jesus no crying he makes.
I love thee, Lord Jesus!
Look down from the sky,
And stay by my side until morning is nigh.

Be near me, Lord Jesus, I ask thee to stay
Close by me for ever, and love me, I pray.
Bless all the dear children in thy tender care,
And fit us for heaven to live with thee there.

"Away in a Manger"
Verses 1-2 attributed to Martin Luther
(1483-1546)
Verse 3 by John T. McFarland (1851-1913)

Father, you have made us for family life, and you call those who are parents to love our children for Jesus' sake. We pray for our own family, and for the families we know best, that this Christmas will be one when there are many spiritual blessings for our children. Amen.

24. JESUS THE NAZARENE

M atthew closes his nativity account with an enigmatic statement: "And he went and lived in a city called Nazareth, so that what was spoken by the prophets might be fulfilled, that he would be called a Nazarene" (Matthew 2:23).

These words have often puzzled careful Bible readers. Search the Old Testament from beginning to end and you will not find the words *he shall be called a Nazarene*.

So how did living in Nazareth fulfil the expectation of the prophets?

We have noticed that Matthew sees prophecy being fulfilled in different ways (1:22; 2:15; 2:17)—sometimes very literally (as in Micah's prophecy of the place of Messiah's birth); at other times by a pattern being filled out that helps us understand the ministry of Jesus (as in the case of the exodus from Egypt).

But what is going on here?

Jewish people, like Matthew and those who first heard his Gospel, loved word plays and puns. (You probably know people like that too!) So, perhaps in calling Jesus a Nazarene, Matthew is playing on the sound of the Hebrew word "branch" (*netser*) used in the messianic prophecy of Isaiah 11:1-2: "There shall come forth a shoot from the stump of Jesse, and *a branch* [*netser*] from his roots shall bear fruit. And the Spirit of the Lord shall rest upon him." In Matthew's own day these words were already being interpreted as a reference to the messianic King. Matthew has been showing us that Jesus was from the "stump" (that is, what remained of the family) of Jesse, King David's father. He was the one the prophets had foretold. Jesus, son of David, son of Jesse—Jesus the Nazarene was Jesus the *Netser-One*!

But there is another possibility. John's Gospel records the somewhat "look-down-my-nose" comment that Nathanael made when he heard that Jesus was from Nazareth: "Can anything good come out of Nazareth?" (John 1:46). Some places have a bad reputation. I was brought up in Glasgow, Scotland's largest city. In my childhood, at least outside of the city itself, "Glasgow" was virtually code language for poverty, slums, litter, alcoholism, and violence. My wife (who attended an all-girls school in another city) was warned by one of her teachers against "boys from Glasgow"! Labelling someone a "Nazarene" gave a similar impression.

So, Matthew is not trying to trick us by saying, *See if you can find this verse in the Old Testament.* He may be playing on the sound of the name of Jesus' hometown. But I suspect he is also saying that the message of the prophets was that the Saviour would not emerge from the

ruling classes, from the royal palaces, or from the power-
ful people. Instead, as Isaiah had specifically said...

> *He grew up before him like a young plant,*
>   *and like a root out of dry ground;*
> *He had no form or majesty that we should look*
> *at him,*
>   *and no beauty that we should desire him.*
>   *(Isaiah 53:2)*

In other words, a "Nazarene-type." Right from his in-
fancy, the child Jesus would give every indication that
he was the Suffering Servant of Isaiah's prophecy. From
the beginning to the end, "though he was in the form
of God ... [he] made himself nothing, taking the form
of a servant ... And being found in human form, he
humbled himself by becoming obedient to the point of
death, even death on a cross" (Philippians 2:6-8).

The great composer Johann Sebastian Bach captured
this aspect of the nativity story when he wove together
his now famous *Christmas Oratorio* for the 1734 Advent
season in the church where he served. In it he sprung a
surprise on the congregation. Bach set the words of a
familiar Advent hymn by Paul Gerhardt, "O Lord, How
Shall I Meet Thee?" to the tune to which the congregation normally sang Gerhardt's Passiontide hymn "O
Sacred Head, Sore Wounded."

A Passion melody in the Christmas story? Bach was a
theologian-in-music. His oratorio expressed the gospel
message: Jesus was the King born in Bethlehem who

would become the Saviour crucified at Calvary. The cross was the destiny of the newborn infant. It is the watermark on every page of the gospel story.

In the same way, Matthew's story—which began with Abraham, in whose seed all nations would be blessed, and was later entwined with the root of David—eventually leads to Jesus, who was "called a Nazarene": the Suffering Servant, prophesied by Isaiah, who was "despised and rejected by men; a man of sorrows, and acquainted with grief." But the deeper truth was that "he was wounded for our transgressions; he was crushed for our iniquities" (Isaiah 53:3, 5).

The Christmas story was heading to the Cross from the very beginning.

Christmas, then, is the dawn of redeeming grace. And as we have seen, Matthew's Gospel ends with the light of God's grace reaching further still, as Jesus the Nazarene—crucified, risen, and about to ascend to the right hand of his Father—tells his followers to "go ... and make disciples of all nations" (Matthew 28:19).

Matthew knew that neither he nor all of the apostles together could personally go to every nation on earth. But his Gospel account could; and so he wrote it. And it has reached us.

We have reflected only on the beginning of Matthew's story. But we have learned enough to know that there is nothing more important in all the world than to welcome Jesus into our lives as Joseph did. There is no journey more significant than to go in search of Christ like the wise men. There is no fellowship more wonderful than to bow with them before Immanuel, God with us. And there is no other Saviour than "the Nazarene" who is our King. Worship is the only present he wants from us. What could be better on Christmas Eve than to give it—to give ourselves—to him?

O Lord, how shall I meet thee,
How welcome thee aright?
Your people long to greet thee,
My hope, my heart's delight!

O sacred head, sore wounded,
With grief and shame weighed down;
Now scornfully surrounded
With thorns thine only crown!

What language shall I borrow
To thank thee, dearest friend,
For this, thy dying sorrow,
Thy pity without end.

O make me thine for ever:
And should I fainting be,
Lord, let me never, never
Outlive my love to thee.

"O Lord, How Shall I Meet Thee?" and
"O Sacred Head, Sore Wounded"
Paul Gerhardt (1606-1676)

Lord Jesus, child of Bethlehem, refugee of Egypt, despised and rejected Nazarene, once crucified but now risen and exalted, thank you for coming for us, living for us, dying for us, and rising again for us. Thank you for the ways in which you have drawn us to seek you and find you. We trust you as our Saviour; we bow before you as our Lord. And this day we offer you the only present you want and that we can give—ourselves. Take us as we are, and make us what you want us to become. We ask it for your name's sake. Amen.

MORE DEVOTIONALS BY
SINCLAIR B. FERGUSON

thegoodbook
COMPANY

BIBLICAL | RELEVANT | ACCESSIBLE

At The Good Book Company, we are dedicated to helping Christians and local churches grow. We believe that God's growth process always starts with hearing clearly what he has said to us through his timeless word—the Bible.

Ever since we opened our doors in 1991, we have been striving to produce Bible-based resources that bring glory to God. We have grown to become an international provider of user-friendly resources to the Christian community, with believers of all backgrounds and denominations using our books, Bible studies, devotionals, evangelistic resources, and DVD-based courses.

We want to equip ordinary Christians to live for Christ day by day, and churches to grow in their knowledge of God, their love for one another, and the effectiveness of their outreach.

Call us for a discussion of your needs or visit one of our local websites for more information on the resources and services we provide.

Your friends at The Good Book Company

thegoodbook.com | thegoodbook.co.uk
thegoodbook.com.au | thegoodbook.co.nz
thegoodbook.co.in